Stalin and Stalinism

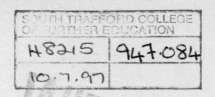

LANCASTER PAMPHLETS

Stalin and Stalinism

Alan Wood

London and New York

First published 1990 by Routledge
11 New Fetter Lane,
London EC4P 4EE

Simultaneously published in the USA and Canada by Routledge
29 West 35th Street, New York, NY 10001

Reprinted in 1993

© 1990 Alan Wood

Photoset by Rowland Phototypesetting Ltd
Bury St Edmunds, Suffolk
Printed in England by Clays Ltd, St Ives plc

British Library Cataloguing in Publication Data
Wood, Alan
Stalin and Stalinism. – (Lancaster pamphlets)
1. Stalinism, History
I.   Title II. Series
335.43

ISBN 0-415-03721-2

Library of Congress Cataloging in Publication Data
Wood, Alan, 1943–
Stalin and Stalinism / Alan Wood.
p.   cm.— (Lancaster pamphlets)
Includes bibliographical references (p.
ISBN 0-415-03721-2
1. Stalin, Joseph, 1879–1953.   2. Heads of state—Soviet Union—
Biography.   3. Soviet Union—Politics and government—1917–1936.
4. Soviet Union—Politics and government—1936–1953.   I. Title.
II Series.
DK268.S8W63   1990
947.084′2′092—dc20
[B]   89-70163   CIP

Contents

Foreword

Lancaster Pamphlets offer concise and up-to-date accounts of major historical topics, primarily for the help of students preparing for Advanced Level examinations, though they should also be of value to those pursuing introductory courses in universities and other institutions of higher education. Without being all-embracing, their aims are to bring some of the central themes or problems confronting students and teachers into sharper focus than the textbook writer can hope to do; to provide the reader with some of the results of recent research which the textbook may not embody; and to stimulate thought about the whole interpretation of the topic under discussion.

At the end of this pamphlet is a list of works, most of them recent or fairly recent, which the writer considers most important for those who wish to study the subject further.

Notes and acknowledgements

i. Russian personal names which are more familiar in their anglicized version have been rendered accordingly; otherwise they have been retained in their original form. This accounts for such apparent inconsistencies as Tsar *Nicholas* I, and *Nikolai* Bukharin; Grand Duke *Michael*, and *Mikhail* Gorbachev.

ii. In the transliteration of Russian technical terms, acronyms, abbreviations, and surnames, a common-sense pattern has been adopted which combines certain features of the standard systems.

iii. Dates before February 1918 are given according to the Julian calendar, until then used in Russia. Thereafter they follow the Gregorian calendar.

iv. St Petersburg was the name of the capital of the Russian Empire until 1914. During the First World War its name was changed to the Russian form – Petrograd. In 1918 Moscow became the new capital, and in 1924 Petrograd was renamed Leningrad.

v. No attempt has been made to psychoanalyse Stalin's character and behaviour, nor are any details given about his personal relationships and family life.

vi. Thanks are due to the series editors, Eric Evans and David King, for their valuable suggestions and encouragement; to John Haywood, for preparing the map on p. xvii; to my colleague Mike Perrins, to my former student Terry Cocks, and to my wife, Iris, for reading and commenting on the text in its preliminary draft; to my youngest daughter, Tanya, for various services rendered.

Alan Wood
University of Lancaster, 1989

Chronological guide

Unless otherwise specifically stated, all entries refer to the life and activities of Stalin.

1879

  9 Dec.   Born in Gori, Georgia.

1888

  Sept.   Begins local elementary school.

1894

  Sept.   Enters Tiflis Orthodox Theological Seminary.

1898   Joins Georgian Marxist political circle, *Messame Dassy*.
                 Founding Congress of Russian Social Democratic Workers' Party (RSDRP) in Minsk.

1899   Expelled from seminary.

1902   Arrested in Batumi for revolutionary activities; exiled to Siberia.

1903   Second Congress of RSDRP; split occurs between Mensheviks and Lenin's Bolsheviks.

1904   Escapes from Siberia and returns to Transcaucasia.

1905   Revolutionary upheavals throughout Russian Empire.

  Dec.   Attends Bolshevik Conference in Finland; meets Lenin for the first time.

1906–12   Active in revolutionary underground; several times arrested, imprisoned, and exiled; present at 1906 and 1907 congresses of RSDRP.

1912

Jan.	Prague Congress of RSDRP; split between Mensheviks and Bolsheviks becomes final; Stalin not present, but made member of Bolshevik Central Committee.
Sept.	Escapes from exile.
Sept.–Dec.	Edits *Pravda*; visits Lenin in Cracow, Poland.

1913

Jan.	Writes first major theoretical work, *Marxism and the National Problem*, on Lenin's suggestion.
Feb.	Returns to St Petersburg; re-arrested.
July.	Exiled to Siberia again.
1913–17	Remains in Siberian exile.
1914	Outbreak of First World War.

1917

Feb.–March.	February Revolution; abdication of Tsar Nicholas II; formation of first Provisional Government and Petrograd Soviet of Workers' and Soldiers' Deputies.
March	Returns from exile; rejoins editorial board of *Pravda*.
April	Lenin returns to Russia from exile in Switzerland.
July	Lenin avoids arrest and goes into hiding in Finland. Stalin becomes Bolsheviks' leading spokesman on Petrograd Soviet and member of party's new Central Committee.
Oct.	Bolsheviks seize power and form Soviet of People's Commissars; Stalin becomes Commissar for Nationalities.

1918

Jan.–March	Supports Lenin's attempts to conclude peace with Germany.
March	Treaty of Brest–Litovsk signed. Civil War gets under way.
June–Oct.	In Tsaritsyn on political mission; clashes with local military commander and with Commissar for War, Trotsky.
1919	RSDRP renamed the All-Russian Communist Party (Bolsheviks); Stalin elected to Politburo and Orgburo.
March	First Congress of Communist International, Moscow.

Oct.–Dec.	Defeat of White forces in south and Siberia; Stalin active on various military fronts.
1921	Tenth Party Congress; inauguration of New Economic Policy.
	Stalin preoccupied with nationalities policies; crushes independent Georgian government.
1922	
April	Elected General Secretary of party Central Committee.
May	Lenin suffers first stroke.
Sept.–Dec.	Lenin quarrels with Stalin over handling of nationalities issue.
Dec.	Formation of Union of Soviet Socialist Republics.
1923	
Jan.	Lenin proposes Stalin's removal from post of General Secretary; suffers second stroke, retires from political life.
1924	
21 Jan.	Death of Lenin. Stalin in charge of funeral arrangements.
April	Publication of *Foundations of Leninism*. Beginnings of the 'cult of Lenin'.
May–Dec.	Anti-Trotsky campaign gathers pace.
1925–6	Develops theory of 'Socialism in One Country'; campaign against Trotsky widens to include Kamenev and Zinoviev.
1927	Trotsky and Zinoviev expelled from the party.
1928	Visits western Siberia and orders forcible requisitioning of grain.
	Inauguration of first five-year plan for the rapid industrialization of the economy.
1929	Announces full-scale collectivization of agriculture; refers to 'liquidation of the kulaks'.
1930	Publication of article, 'Dizzy with Success', criticizing over-zealous collectivization methods.
1932	First five-year plan completed in four years.
	Formula of 'socialist realism' in literature adopted.
1933	Adolf Hitler becomes Chancellor of Germany.
	Famine in the Ukraine.
1934	
Jan.–Feb.	Seventeenth Party Congress – 'Congress of Victors'.

	Yagoda becomes head of NKVD.
1 Dec.	Assassination of Kirov heralds beginning of purge.
1935	Kamenev and Zinoviev arrested in connection with Kirov's murder.
	Adoption of policy of Popular Fronts against fascism in Europe.
1936	The 'Great Terror' gets under way.
June	Public show trial, conviction, and execution of Kamenev, Zinoviev, and others.
August	Yezhov replaces Yagoda as head of NKVD.
Nov.	Publication of new Constitution of USSR, proclaimed as 'the most democratic in the world'.
1937	Height of the terror; second major show trial and execution of the accused; purge of the officer corps of Soviet armed forces.
	End of second five-year plan.
1938	
March	Trial and execution of Bukharin and others.
Oct.	Munich agreement on dismemberment of Czechoslovakia.
Dec.	Beria replaces Yezhov as head of NKVD.
1939	
March	Purges declared to be over.
Sept.	Germany invades Poland; beginning of Second World War.
	Soviet troops occupy eastern Poland.
Nov.	Soviet Union attacks Finland; start of the 'Winter War'.
1940	Stalin becomes Chairman of Council of People's Commissars (head of government).
March	End of war with Finland.
July	Soviet occupation of the Baltic states.
20 August	Assassination of Trotsky in Mexico.
1941	
22 June	Operation Barbarossa – German invasion of USSR.
Oct.	Siege of Leningrad commences; battle for Moscow launched.
Dec.	Soviet counter-offensive; Moscow saved.

1942

June–August	Soviet forces retreat in south; battle of Stalingrad commences.
Nov.	Soviet troops cut off German 6th Army at Stalingrad.

1943

Jan.	Relief of Leningrad.
Feb.	Germans surrender at Stalingrad.
March	Stalin assumes rank of Marshal.
Nov.	Kiev retaken by Red Army. Teheran Conference (Stalin, Roosevelt, Churchill).

1944

June	Allied landings in Normandy.
July–Dec.	Soviet forces advance across eastern and south-eastern Europe.

1945

Jan.	Red Army enters Warsaw.
Feb.	Yalta Conference (Stalin, Roosevelt, Churchill).
May	Red Army reaches Berlin.
8/9 May	Germany surrenders; end of war in Europe.
June	Stalin adopts title of Generalissimo.
July–August	Potsdam Conference (Stalin, Truman, Attlee).
6 August	USA drops atomic bomb on Hiroshima.
9 August	Atomic bomb dropped on Nagasaki. USSR declares war on Japan.
2 Sept.	End of war with Japan.

1946

March	Announcement of fourth five-year plan for national reconstruction. Churchill's 'Iron Curtain' speech at Fulton, Missouri.
August	'Zhdanov decrees' on literary and cultural conformity.

1948

June	Beginning of the Berlin blockade. Break between USSR and Yugoslavia.
August	Death of Zhdanov; beginning of the 'Leningrad Affair'.

1949

April	Establishment of North Atlantic Treaty

	Organization (NATO).
Oct.	Victory of Chinese communists; establishment of People's Republic of China.
Dec.	Stalin's seventieth birthday celebrated with lavish festivities.
1952	Nineteenth Party Congress.
1953	
Jan.	Discovery of so-called 'Doctors' Plot'.
5 March	Death of Stalin.
Sept.	USSR announces possession of the H-bomb.
1953–6	Period of 'Collective Leadership'.
1956	
Feb.	Twentieth Party Congress; Khrushchev denounces Stalin's 'cult of personality' in 'secret speech'.
1961	
Oct.	Twenty-second Party Congress; 'de-Stalinization' campaign at its height; Stalin's body removed from mausoleum.
1964	
Oct.	Khrushchev removed from power.
1964–82	General Secretaryship of Leonid Brezhnev, now referred to in USSR as the 'era of stagnation'; criticism of Stalin muted.
1985	Mikhail Gorbachev becomes General Secretary of Soviet Communist Party; launches campaign of *glasnost* and *perestroika*, including radical re-examination of Stalin era.
1989	Collapse of communist governments throughout eastern Europe.

Glossary of Russian technical terms and abbreviations

apparat	Soviet party or government bureaucracy
apparatchik	a party or government functionary; member of the *apparat*
Bolshevik	originally, a member of Lenin's 'hard-line' faction of the RSDRP
cadres	full-time professional party activists
Cheka	Extraordinary Commission for Struggle with Counter-revolution and Sabotage, established in 1917, the first Soviet political police
Comintern	Third (Communist) International, established in 1919, dissolved in 1943
dacha	a Russian country house
Duma	elected state assembly with severely limited constitutional powers, 1906–17
glasnost	'openness' or 'publicity'; public access to information
GULag	Main Prison Camp Administration
intelligentsia	in Soviet usage, professionally qualified cultural and scientific workers
KGB	Committee for State Security
kolkhoz (nik)	collective farm(er)
kulak	a 'rich' peasant (NB: a very elastic term, used in the 1930s to denote peasants who opposed collectivization)

Menshevik	member of the moderate faction of the RSDRP
Messame Dassy	(Georgian) 'The Third Group', a Marxist revolutionary circle in Georgia, joined by Stalin
MTS	Machine Tractor Station; state-controlled supplier of agricultural machinery to collective farms
NEP	New Economic Policy; limited free-market economy operating during 1920s
Nepmen	private entrepreneurs active during NEP
NKVD	People's Commissariat for Internal Affairs, the 'ministry' responsible for Stalin's secret-police operations
Orgburo	Organizational Bureau, central party organ in charge of personnel and administration, abolished in 1952
perestroika	'restructuring' – term used to describe Gorbachev's programme of political and economic reform
Politburo	Political Bureau, supreme policy-making body of the Soviet Communist Party
Pravda	literally, 'Truth', the central Bolshevik, later Communist, party newspaper
Proletkult	'Proletarian culture', campaign in 1920s to promote a specifically industrial working-class culture
rabfak	'workers' faculty'; established in the 1920s to prepare workers and peasants for higher education
Rabkrin	Workers' and Peasants' Inspectorate, organ of state control during 1920s; Stalin was briefly its chairman
Rabochii Put'	'The Workers' Road', Bolshevik party newspaper published during 1917
RSDRP	Russian Social Democratic Workers' Party
soviet	literally, 'council'; since the Revolution, usually referring to central and local government councils
Sovnarkom	Council of People's Commissars – the first Soviet government, set up in October 1917
spetsy	'specialists', especially 'bourgeois specialists', i.e. professionally qualified people employed in various capacities in the 1920s
Yezhovshchina	term applied to Stalin's terror campaign of the 1930s, after Yezhov, head of the NKVD

Zhdanovshchina term applied to the period of extreme cultural repression in USSR in late 1940s, after senior Politburo member, Andrei Zhdanov

Author's preface

This pamphlet was written during March 1989, before the full extent of the dramatic revolutionary changes which shook eastern Europe at the end of that year could reasonably have been anticipated. One after another, the Communist governments of Poland, Hungary, Czechoslovakia, the German Democratic Republic, and Romania have been forced from office by mass popular upheavals. The most potent symbol of the post-war division of Europe, the Berlin Wall, has come tumbling down and events have moved rapidly towards the reunification of the two Germanys. Heads of government, presidents, and Communist Party leaders throughout the region – men who had made their careers by serving the system originally imposed on their countries by Joseph Stalin – have been sacked, humiliated, arrested and, in the case of Romania's Nicolae Ceausescu, shot.

The Soviet Union itself has witnessed rapid political and economic reform: the restructuring of central and local government bodies; the emergence of independent political movements; the public discussion of the desirability of a multi-party political system and the abandonment of the vanguard role of the Soviet Communist Party; vociferous and even violent calls for the national independence of the constituent republics of the USSR, which has already led to the declaration of independence by Lithuania, in March 1990. Together with the toleration of Russian religious revivalism and the virtual emasculation of the Warsaw Pact as a serious military threat to the West, all of these events and movements in a sense represent the death throes of the system established first in the USSR and then extended into eastern and central Europe by the once Soviet dictator, Joseph Stalin, the subject of this brief study. That is why, in order to appreciate the real historic significance of these recent events, it is essential first to understand the political, historical, and ideological phenomena discussed in the following pages and signified by the title of this booklet – *Stalin and Stalinism*.

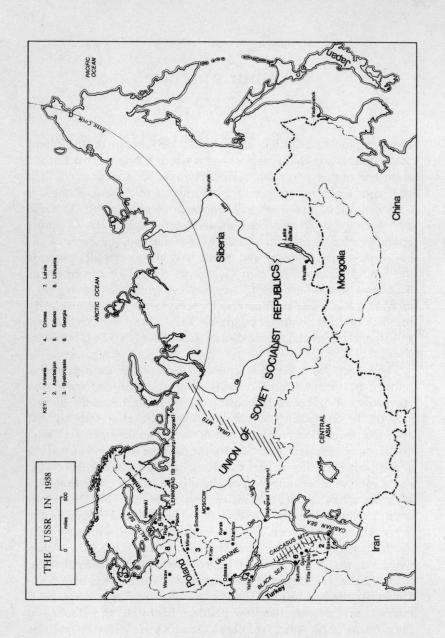

THE USSR IN 1938

0 miles 500

KEY: 1. Armenia 4. Crimea 7. Latvia
2. Azerbaijan 5. Estonia 8. Lithuania
3. Byelorussia 6. Georgia

PACIFIC OCEAN

Japan

Vladivostok

China

Mongolia

Arctic Circle

Siberia

Yakutsk

Lena

Lake Baikal

Irkutsk

ARCTIC OCEAN

UNION OF SOVIET SOCIALIST REPUBLICS

Ob

URAL MTS

CENTRAL ASIA

Finland

LENINGRAD (St Petersburg/Petrograd)

Helsinki

Tallinn

BALTIC SEA

Riga

Pskov

Smolensk

MOSCOW

Kursk

Kharkov

Volga

Don

Stalingrad (Tsaritsyn)

CASPIAN SEA

Iran

Warsaw

Poland

Minsk

Kiev

UKRAINE

Odessa

Yalta

BLACK SEA

Batumi

Gori

Tiflis (Tbilisi)

Baku

CAUCASUS MTS

Turkey

Introduction

During the 1980s two new terms entered the political vocabulary of the world. These are the Russian words *glasnost* and *perestroika*, the first meaning something like 'openness', 'frankness', or 'publicity', and the second meaning literally 'restructuring'. They began to be used with increasing frequency in connection with the programme of economic, political, and cultural reform inaugurated in the Soviet Union after Mikhail Gorbachev became the General Secretary of the country's Communist Party in 1985. Because of the tremendous international power and importance of the Soviet Union, these changes will have wide ramifications not only for the citizens of the USSR, but for the rest of the world as well, as the astonishing political upheavals throughout eastern Europe in 1989 have demonstrated. This is not the right place to discuss these developments, but what is important to realize is that when one hears or reads of *perestroika* today, what is actually being 'restructured' is the political, social, economic, and ideological system which was created by the man who ruled the Soviet Union for twenty-five years (1928–53) as its unchallenged dictator – Joseph Stalin.

For a quarter of a century the entire life of the largest country in the world and of millions of its citizens was dominated by a political leader who was once described by the Yugoslav communist Milovan Djilas as 'the greatest criminal in history', in whom was combined 'the criminal senselessness of a Caligula with the refinement of a Borgia and the brutality of a Tsar Ivan the Terrible'. How was it that

1

the initial enthusiasms and aspirations of the Russian Revolution in 1917 which promised a more just and humane society became distorted into a totalitarian despotism which trampled on justice and humanity and plunged the Soviet Union into a nightmare of terror which reached almost genocidal proportions? Was Stalinism the logical and inevitable consequence of Lenin's original revolutionary policies or, on the contrary, was it a grotesque perversion of Bolshevism, and was Stalin himself 'the gravedigger of the Revolution'? The impressive economic achievements of the Stalin era cannot be denied, turning Russia from an underdeveloped, peasant society into an industrial giant and a military superpower capable of withstanding the onslaught of Hitler's armies in 1941–5 and terrifying the west during the years of the Cold War. As Stalin himself remarked, he found the country with the wooden plough and left her with the atomic bomb. But all this was accomplished at a terrible price in human misery and suffering. Could it have been achieved by any other means than the oppressive weapons of coercion and control which Stalin wielded through the apparatus of a police state? Were there other, alternative paths of economic development? Were the famines and forced-labour camps, the millions of exiles and executions essential to the building of 'Socialism in One Country'? And how did one man come to wield such terrifying power over the Communist Party and the Soviet people?

For two generations it was impossible not only to answer but even to ask such questions inside the Soviet Union. For nearly a decade after his death, Stalin's embalmed corpse lay next to that of Lenin in the mausoleum on Red Square, still an object of public veneration and pilgrimage even after the then Soviet leader, Nikita Khrushchev, had delivered his startling attack on his dead master in 1956. And it took another two and a half decades before the 'accursed questions' of the Soviet Union's Stalinist past could be properly investigated and opened up for public debate and professional examination by historians, politicians, journalists, and creative writers without fear of official disapproval or worse. It is difficult nowadays to pick up a serious newspaper, magazine, or journal in the Soviet Union which does not contain somewhere in its pages an article either directly or indirectly concerned with some aspect of Stalin's bloody regime or his ambiguous legacy. There is an atmosphere of intellectual curiosity, agonizing self-questioning, critical re-evaluation and often acrimonious accusation in an attempt to fill in the 'blank spots' in Russia's recent history which even three or four years ago would

2

have been unthinkable. People are no longer afraid to ask, but no one is yet really sure of the answers – not even the professional historians who are in the front line of the attack on the now discredited official versions of the historical 'truth'. Because of the uncertainty, in 1988 Russian History examinations were cancelled in Soviet schools, and in the same year a leading Moscow newspaper carried a cartoon in which a history teacher with textbook in hand is asking a young pupil, 'Do you want to know what it says in the books, or do you want to know the truth?'

It is, in short, an exciting time to be studying Russian history, and also an extremely apposite moment to extend the list of Lancaster Pamphlets with this short examination of the way in which the son of a drunken Georgian cobbler came to be ruler of the Soviet Union and arguably the most powerful, malevolent, and controversial political figure of the twentieth century.

1
The historical setting

Background

The internal social and economic conditions, the oppressive political system, the national tensions and the class conflicts within the Russian Empire which led to the revolutions of 1917 have been described elsewhere in this series.* However, it is worth recalling some of the salient features of the tsarist social and political order into which Joseph Stalin was born and in which he served his revolutionary apprenticeship.

At the end of the nineteenth century the Russian Empire was the largest continuous land–empire in the world, covering approximately one-sixth of the earth's land surface. In 1897 it contained a population of over 125 million people, of which only two-fifths were Russian. The other 60 per cent was made up of a multinational, multilingual, and multireligious conglomeration of Slavs, Jews, Balts, Finns, Georgians, Armenians, Azeris, Turkic-speaking Muslim peoples of Central Asia, and a whole patchwork of aboriginal ethnic groups and tribes in Siberia and the Far East. Many of them suffered from various forms of racial discrimination and religious persecution and actively struggled to liberate themselves from Russian imperialism. Stalin, himself a non-Russian, made the nationalities problem of the Russian Empire one of his special areas of

* Alan Wood, *The Origins of the Russian Revolution 1861–1917*, Lancaster Pamphlets, Methuen, London, 1987.

expertise, and it was in fact as People's Commissar for Nationalities that he made his political debut in the very first Soviet government.

From 1894 to 1917 this empire was ruled over by Tsar Nicholas I, the last representative of the Romanov dynasty which had governed Russia for the past three centuries as absolute autocrats. Until as late as 1906 the country had neither parliamentary institutions nor legal political parties through which the will, or even the grievances, of the people could be expressed. Members of the government were appointed by the emperor and were directly responsible to his person; he consequently had the power to hire and fire them at will. There were no constitutional constraints on the tsars' authority and even the Fundamental Laws of the Russian Empire which were promulgated after the revolutionary upheavals of 1905 stated unequivocally that the God-given supreme power lay with Sovereign Autocrat. Russia therefore had a long and deeply ingrained tradition of political subservience to a single, all-powerful ruler.

The overwhelming majority of Nicholas's subjects (over 80 per cent) were peasants, with only 13 per cent of the population living in towns or cities. Despite a remarkable burst of industrial growth at the turn of the century, Russia was still therefore an unmistakably agrarian society. Most of the peasants lived in village communes which closely regulated their activities and in many areas periodically redistributed land allotments among the peasant households. This redistributional system of land tenure and usage, combined with primitive farming techniques and a rapidly expanding rural population, led to agricultural underproduction, land hunger, and occasional famine. The emancipation of the peasantry from serfdom in 1861 had miserably failed to solve the country's agrarian problems, and in the early years of the twentieth century there was a recrudescence of peasant violence which finally forced the government to introduce a new series of reforms in the village economy. The reforms were, however, 'too little and too late' and the rebellious peasantry continued to be a major thorn in the government's flesh before, during, and until well after the 1917 Revolution. Stalin was later to tackle the peasant problem in his own inimical and inimitable manner, with devastating consequences.

Stalin's great rival, Leon Trotsky (1879–1940), described the Russian peasantry as 'the subsoil of the Revolution'. The topsoil was provided by the industrial working class, or proletariat. Although only small in numbers compared with the peasants, the Russian workers had developed in a remarkably short period of time into a highly militant and class-conscious force in both economic and political terms. This was vividly demonstrated by the general strike of October 1905 which paralysed the country's economy and administration, and by the formation of the St Petersburg *Soviet* (Council) of workers' deputies, a kind of popular parliament which commanded the loyalty of the capital's workers in defiance of the bewildered government during the nationwide disorders of that year. The radicalization of the working class was partly a consequence of the objective conditions in which they lived and worked, and partly a result of the propaganda and organization of Marxist revolutionary activists who welcomed the development of capitalist relationships in the Russian economy and looked beyond the overthrow of tsarism by a 'bourgeois-democratic revolution' to the time when the working class would rise and destroy capitalism and the bourgeois state in the 'proletarian-socialist revolution'.

In 1903 a newly formed underground revolutionary party, the Russian Social Democratic Workers' Party (RSDRP), had split into two mutually antagonistic factions known as the Bolsheviks ('majority-ites') and the Mensheviks ('minority-ites'). The Bolsheviks were led by Vladimir Ilyich Lenin (1870–1924), who in a pamphlet written in 1902 had argued for a disciplined, centralized party organization of professional revolutionaries which would form the leadership – the 'vanguard' – of the proletariat in the socialist revolution. The Mensheviks, headed by Julius Martov (1873–1923), were in favour of a broader, mass party and generally held more moderate views on most practical and ideological issues than Lenin's hard-line Bolsheviks. It was of course the Bolsheviks who were to seize political power in the name of the workers' soviets in October 1917, and it was this party's bureaucratic machinery which was later to serve as the vehicle for Stalin's political ambition in his seemingly inexorable rise to supreme power during the 1920s.

Revolution

The many conflicts and contradictions at work within the tsarist social and political structure were placed under intolerable strain as a result of Russia's entry into the First World War in August 1914. The short-lived jingoistic euphoria which initially greeted the declaration of hostilities rapidly gave way to a mood of frustration, despair, and anger at the government's bungling mismanagement of the military and civilian war effort. Millions were conscripted and marched into

7

the trenches of eastern Europe with only a rudimentary training and often with inadequate weapons and ammunition. At the front, whole armies of these 'peasants in uniform' were defeated, decimated, or taken as prisoners of war by the superior German and Austrian forces. In the rear, the unpopularity of the tsar and his government was exacerbated by Nicholas's foolish decision to take over personal command of the Russian army, and by the public scandal caused by the royal family's involvement in the sordid Rasputin affair. Members of the elected national assembly, the State Duma, called on the emperor to dismiss his incompetent ministers and replace them with a government which would enjoy the confidence of the people. Secret-police reports reinforced the politicians' fears with daily information of violent incidents on the streets and prophetic warnings about the increasingly revolutionary temper of the masses. Nicholas, however, paid no heed as the chorus of popular disaffection and war-weariness reached a dramatic crescendo in the early weeks of 1917.

At the end of February striking workers, demonstrating women, and mutinous soldiers held the capital in their grip and the authorities seemed powerless to re-establish order and control. The tsar, foiled by railway workers from returning to Petrograd (as St Petersburg had now been renamed) from army headquarters and faced with increasing pressure from his senior military advisers to step down, finally bowed to the inevitable and abdicated the throne in favour of his brother, Grand Duke Michael. Michael refused, and the three-hundred-year rule of the Romanov tsars was at a sudden end. The political vacuum created by the collapse of the autocracy was quickly though confusingly filled by the creation of two independent organs of authority, the so-called Provisional Government, composed of moderate Duma politicians, and the Petrograd Soviet of Workers' and Soldiers' Deputies, which represented the interests of the revolutionary workers and troops of the capital. Similar soviets were soon established throughout the country, replacing in a somewhat anarchical fashion the now defunct authority of the imperial administration. This situation was later described by Lenin as one of 'dual power'.

The socialist parties, including both Bolsheviks and Mensheviks, naturally welcomed the collapse of tsarism as the predicted 'bourgeois-democratic revolution', and although their attitude to the relationship between the Provisional Government and the Petrograd Soviet was somewhat equivocal, none of the parties' leaders was yet thinking seriously about the possibility of a 'pro-letarian-socialist revolution' in the immediate future. Stalin was one of the first senior Bolsheviks to return to Petrograd from exile after the February Revolution, but it was really the arrival of Lenin on 3 April which introduced a new and ultimately decisive factor into the highly volatile political atmosphere. The Bolshevik leader announced that there should be no collaboration with the bourgeois government, no reunification of the Bolshevik and Menshevik parties, and no further participation by Russia in the imperialist war. He characterized the current situation as a period of transition from the bourgeois-democratic to the proletarian-socialist phase of the revolutionary process and called on the party to prepare the masses for an armed insurrection which would transfer 'all power to the soviets'. Lenin's *April Theses*, as his proposals came to be called, were initially repudiated by other leading Bolsheviks, including Stalin, but eventually became accepted as the party's 'order of the day'.

It was not, however, for another six months that circumstances were deemed to be sufficiently favourable to put that order into effect. Only in September, after the collapse of two Provisional Governments, continuing military disasters at the front, an abortive right-wing coup led by the army's commander-in-chief, widespread peasant disorders, and a renewed upswing in Bolshevik support and membership on the Petrograd Soviet, did Lenin decide to strike. Leon Trotsky had joined the Bolsheviks in August and was now chairman of both the Soviet and its Military Revolutionary Committee, which controlled the garrison's troops. On the night of 24–5 October platoons of armed workers, soldiers, and sailors under the command of the Military Revolutionary Committee took over key installations in the capital. On the following night they attacked the Winter Palace and arrested the members of the last Provisional Government. The insurrection was later announced at a meeting of the second All-Russian Congress of Soviets, which was then in session; and, following the withdrawal of Mensheviks and the peasant-based Socialist Revolutionary Party delegates, the now Bolshevik-dominated congress voted into office a new revolution-ary government called the Council of People's Commissars, or *Sovnarkom*. Lenin was its chairman, and included in its initial mem-bership with a brand new portfolio was his loyal lieutenant, Joseph Stalin.

Four more years of bloody civil war were to elapse before the Red

Army's victory over the counter-revolutionary Whites and the interventionist forces of their foreign backers finally established Soviet power throughout most of the old Russian Empire. Another year later, in 1922, Stalin was elected to the party office which he would use to make that empire his own. But how was it that this little-known revolutionary from Georgia come to be appointed General Secretary of the All-Russian Communist Party (Bolsheviks)?

2

The underground revolutionary

Schooling

Lying just beyond the spectacular Caucasus Mountains on the broad isthmus between the Black Sea and the Caspian Sea, the ancient Orthodox Christian kingdom of Georgia had been absorbed into the Russian Empire in the late eighteenth and early nineteenth centuries. Russian tutelage was initially welcomed as it afforded the Georgian people a measure of protection from their traditional Muslim enemies, Persia and the Ottoman Empire. As the nineteenth century progressed the Russian colonial administration introduced a process of gradual industrialization, economic modernization, education, and urbanization which stimulated the growth of a vigorous nationalist movement among the Georgian intelligentsia. The fact that most native Georgians were at the bottom of the social heap while Armenians and Russians dominated respectively the commercial middle classes and the governing bureaucracy meant that nationalist sentiments were closely bound up with social divisions and class-consciousness. Socialism and nationalism were therefore natural allies in the struggle against the Russian imperial regime. For this reason many young Georgian radicals, as well as Jews and Poles, came to play a leading role in the all-Russian Marxist revolutionary movement in the early years of the twentieth century, and it was out of their ranks that Stalin was to emerge as one of the most powerful dictators of that century. His future eminence, however, was belied by his obscure origins.

11

He was born Iosif Vissarionovich Djugashvili on 9 December 1879 in the small town of Gori, about sixty kilometres west of the Georgian capital, Tiflis, now known as Tbilisi. He spent his infancy with his impoverished parents in a ramshackle hovel which also served as his shoemaker father's workshop. Many years later the place of his humble nativity was to be refurbished, immured within a magnificent, marble-colonnaded pavilion, and turned into a national shrine. Very little of any significance is known about his early childhood and it was therefore in all probability totally unremarkable. We know that he was a generally robust, intelligent, and devout young boy, though short in stature and facially scarred by the pit-marks of an early smallpox attack. He was also slightly lame in his left arm, though sources vary as to the cause. His father was something of a drunkard and in 1884 he left his failed cobbler's business to find employment as a worker in a Tiflis shoe factory. Stalin could therefore claim both artisanal and proletarian parentage. Rather than following his father's footsteps into the shoe trade, little Joseph ('Soso') was very fortunate, as the child of near-paupers, to be enrolled at the local elementary school run by the Orthodox Church. By all accounts he was a bright, diligent pupil and eventually completed his course with sufficient distinction for his teachers to recommend his matriculation into the Tiflis Orthodox Theological Seminary, one of the foremost higher-educational institutions in the whole Transcaucasian region.

The move to the capital (in 1894) was to be a momentous step for the young Djugashvili. In the absence of any university in the area, the Tiflis Seminary attracted many of the most intelligent and independent-minded youth of Georgia into its austere surroundings, where a highly rigorous, if naturally heavily ecclesiastical, education was to be acquired. Tiflis was also then the centre of Georgian intellectual unrest, where narrow national dissidence jostled with a growing awareness of more cosmopolitan radical philosophies through the medium of the Russian language. As part of the St Petersburg government's heavy-handed campaign of 'Russification', restrictions on the use of native languages in the non-Russian borderlands and the compulsory use of Russian in many schools and official institutions were widespread. While the authorities hoped that this would result in a greater degree of cultural, intellectual, and political conformity, it also had the unlooked-for consequence of making available to a wider readership not only the works of Russian authors, but also Russian translations of the artistic, scientific, secular, and subversive literature of the west. Although such books were banned to the seminarists, it was through his illicit reading of proscribed texts from the city library that the future Stalin first came into conflict with the seminary authorities. A series of punishments failed to dampen his intellectual curiosity and served only to reinforce the spirit of rebelliousness and anti-authoritarianism now growing inside him. The combination of resentment at his personal treatment and the actual contents of the forbidden literature gradually caused him to question not only the authority of the monks and priests who taught him, but also the very religious principles on which their teaching was based. Exactly when Djugashvili abandoned his faith in Christianity is as unclear as the precise timing of his espousal of revolutionary Marxism as his new, alternative orthodoxy, but it was certainly some time during his five years at the Tiflis Seminary, from which he was duly expelled in May 1899.

The official reason for his expulsion was *not* the dissemination of Marxist propaganda, as he was later to maintain; but obviously his deteriorating conduct and academic performance were not unlinked to his increasing involvement in illegal political activities among the capital's radical intelligentsia and working class. His experience at the seminary was not, however, wasted. Throughout his life the former theological seminarist can be detected in his rigid dogmatism, his rhetorical and literary style, his capacity for diligent and repetitive work, and also in his duplicity and deceitfulness – first developed in his relations with the seminary authorities and later to became one of the hallmarks of his political style. Soso Djugashvili's formal education was now over; his political education in the revolutionary underground was just about to begin.

Struggle

In 1898 the first, founding congress of the Marxist Russian Social Democratic Workers' Party was held in the town of Minsk in Byelorussia. Only a handful of delegates attended and it achieved almost nothing in concrete results. It was, however, one of the first, hesitant steps of the infant party which was soon to grow into such a potent force in Russian history. In the same year Djugashvili joined a small social-democratic organization in Tiflis called *Messame Dassy* ('The Third Group'). Of course the 19-year-old seminary student had only a rudimentary knowledge of Marxist philosophy, and his receptiveness to socialism was the result more of an instinctive awareness and practical experience of the Georgian workers' grievances than of an intellectual understanding of political and economic theory. In the words of one of his biographers, 'his socialism was cold, sober and rough', and stemmed not from sentiment, moral indignation, or book-learning but from the personal circumstances of his boyhood and youth among the disadvantaged and exploited lower classes of Georgian society. It came therefore not from the heart or the mind, but from the gut.

Although he had previously frequented radical discussion circles, membership of The Third Group gave the future Stalin his first experience of practical propaganda work among the Tiflis proletariat. As this would certainly bring him to the attention of the police, he needed to adopt a pseudonym and so chose the name of a Georgian romantic literary hero, 'Koba'. This was the first of many aliases he assumed before the name Stalin (from the Russian word for steel – *stal'*) finally stuck. For the next two or three years Koba/Djugashvili was active in propaganda, agitational, and organizational work both in Tiflis and in the Black Sea coastal town of Batumi, always taking a hard, militant line in any theoretical or practical disputes with his comrades and simultaneously deepening his understanding of the ideological dimensions of the struggle. In 1902 he was arrested, imprisoned, and exiled to eastern Siberia, from where he escaped and made his way back to Georgia in 1904.

During his absence the second congress of the RSDRP had taken place, at which the fateful split between the Bolsheviks and the Mensheviks occurred. Koba was probably unfamiliar with the niceties of the dispute which had caused the division, but temperamentally and intuitively he was more inclined to the Bolshevik camp, unlike the majority of the more moderate Georgian social democrats, many of whom, like N. S. Chkheidze (1864–1926) and I. G. Tsereteli (1881–1960), later became prominent among the leadership of the Mensheviks. The fact that the Bolshevik social democrats were in a minority in Transcaucasia meant that the somewhat abrasive and individualistic Koba acquired a high profile among them and soon came to the attention of the party's national leadership.

The first meeting between Lenin and Stalin took place at a party conference in Finland in December 1905, though there is no evidence that the young Georgian activist made any great impression on the Bolshevik leader. In the following year a so-called 'unification congress' of the party's Menshevik and Bolshevik factions convened in Stockholm, and once more Koba made the journey north, the first time the 26-year-old had set foot outside the Russian Empire. Here, too, he made his maiden speech to a party congress, asserting his individualism by criticizing both the Menshevik and Bolshevik positions on the agrarian question, but otherwise toeing a strictly Leninist line. In the spring of 1907 he once again attended the party congress, this time in London, and although he took no active part in the proceedings his repeated presence among Lenin's supporters at these meetings was beginning to establish him as an apparently consistent and reliable opponent of Menshevism, which was more than could be said for the maverick Leon Trotsky. Stalin would later contrast his own early loyalty to the Bolshevik cause with Trotsky's theoretical disputes with Lenin, to great political advantage.

Needless to say, neither the 1906 nor the 1907 congress succeeded in forging the reunification of the two factions, and they continued to be divided on a whole range of internal ideological and organizational issues which consumed much time and energy over the ensuing decade. Apart from the fundamental differences over the role of the party and the strategy of revolution, there were two particularly contentious problems over which there could be no agreement. One was the so-called 'liquidator' debate. The question was whether, now that the revolutionary events of 1905 had created a more liberal political climate with free elections to the State Duma and legal political parties, there was any longer any need to maintain a clandestine revolutionary underground organization or, on the contrary, it could be 'liquidated', i.e. dismantled. Most Mensheviks favoured its liquidation, while Lenin and the Bolsheviks insisted that the undercover network of agents and their covert operations be maintained. The second issue concerned the question of 'expropriations'. This was the euphemism used to describe the policy of acquiring party funds by means of illicit, even criminal, activities, including the robbing of state banks. As on the liquidator matter, the Mensheviks preferred to operate entirely within the legal framework, whereas the less scrupulous Bolsheviks considered it quite legitimate in the revolutionary cause to expropriate by all available means funds which they believed had in any case been expropriated from the toiling masses in the first place. Consequently the Bolsheviks continued to enjoy the proceeds of the strong-arm tactics of their 'fighting squads'. The expropriation campaign affected Stalin in particular as the Caucasus, with its mountainous terrain and long tradition of brigandage, was a favourite region for acts of violent revolutionary banditry. One of the most notorious exploits was a brazen and bloodthirsty attack on a coachful of money bound for the Tiflis State Bank in June 1907 which resulted in several killings and a haul of over 300,000 rubles. The raid was led by an old comrade of Stalin, a flamboyant Armenian terrorist known as 'Kamo' Ter Petrossian; and although it is unlikely that Stalin himself had any direct hand in the robbery, intensified police activity in Tiflis following the incident possibly influenced his decision to shift his operational base from Tiflis to the centre of the Russian oil industry, Baku, on the shores of the Caspian Sea.

The police in Baku, however, were no less vigilant than elsewhere, and in March 1908 Koba was once more arrested and sent for another spell of internal exile from which he escaped even more easily than the first time and returned to Baku. He was soon re-arrested and escorted back to complete his sentence. On his release in 1911 he decided to move to St Petersburg but was promptly expelled from the capital. In the next year he was appointed a member of the Bolshevik Central Committee following the 'Bolsheviks-only' party congress in Prague at which the divorce between Lenin's party and the Mensheviks became absolute. Despite later attempts at reconciliation, the Bolsheviks and Mensheviks were now effectually two separate parties, with separate policies and separate organizations. His elevation to the party leadership was no doubt a reward for the uncompromisingly anti-Menshevik line pursued by Stalin, as he now came invariably to be called. At about the same time he also joined the editorial board of the party newspaper, *Pravda*, on which he continued to argue forcefully against those who still retained hopes of a Menshevik–Bolshevik reconciliation. After another brush with the law and yet another escape from Siberian exile, Stalin was now entrusted by Lenin with a major piece of theoretical writing. This was a long essay on 'Marxism and the National Problem', which was published in 1913 and firmly established the Georgian Bolshevik as the party's leading theoretician on the relationship between class, nationalism, and the revolution.

Like other leading Bolsheviks, however, he was not around to witness or participate in the actual revolution which broke out in February 1917. In February 1913 the police had caught up with him yet again and this time decided to banish him to a remote spot in northern Siberia beyond the Arctic Circle. Although he was later allowed to reside further south, he remained in his desolate Siberian exile until the authority of the tsarist police who expelled him collapsed in the ruins of the regime they served.

1917

Like hundreds of other political victims of the Siberian exile system, Stalin immediately seized the opportunity presented by the February Revolution to return as quickly as possible to European Russia and join in the fray. When he arrived in Petrograd on 12 March the political situation was understandably complex and confused. In addition to the confrontational alliance between the Provisional Government and the Soviet (i.e. 'dual power'), the unexpected abdication of the tsar had thrown up a number of urgent issues which exercised all the parties of the left. The most pressing of these were the question of Russia's continuing participation in the war; the possibility of bringing about the reunification of the RSDRP; and the problem of how much support should be given by the socialists to the bourgeois Provisional Government. Initially, the Bolshevik newspaper, *Pravda*, which was being run by three fairly junior party activists, adopted a basically tough attitude on all three questions. However, with the arrival of Stalin and another senior member of the party's Central Committee, G. E. Zinoviev (1883–1936), the editorial line shifted to a more conciliatory position which reflected the generally-held assumption in the party that the revolution would not swiftly transcend the limits of bourgeois democracy. Stalin's personal position was somewhat equivocal: while rejecting the hard-left line, he did not go so far as to embrace the policy either of 'revolutionary defencism', i.e. continuing to fight imperial Germany, or of political collaboration with the Mensheviks and the Provisional Government. Whether this was owing to lack of conviction or to political calculation is difficult to determine.

Even after Lenin's return and the enunciation of the *April Theses*, Stalin did not immediately throw his weight behind the startling new initiative, but before very long force of circumstances made him Lenin's virtual spokesman in the capital. The decisive factor promoting Stalin to his new eminence within the party was the decision of the Provisional Government's new Prime Minister, Alexander Kerensky (1881–1970), to arrest the Bolshevik leaders, including Lenin, in the aftermath of violent demonstrations in July which greeted yet another Russian military débâcle at the front. In the event Lenin decided not to submit to arrest, and instead went into hiding across the Finnish border. However, he and several other prominent Bolsheviks who *were* arrested, as well as Trotsky who had recently declared his solidarity with them, were now temporarily *hors de combat*, and in their absence Stalin thereby acquired a new authority. He was now not only a member of the Central Committee; he was also still a deputy on the Petrograd Soviet and editor of the party's newspaper (renamed *Rabochii Put'* – 'The Workers' Road'). Lacking the flamboyance, charisma, or erudition of the Bolsheviks' intellectual elite, Stalin nevertheless played a vital role during the next few weeks in the day-to-day routine work of organizing committees, cadres, and caucuses, as well as editing *Rabochii Put'* and generally keeping things going at a time when party fortunes were at a low ebb.

It is impossible to say whether this led to any resentment on Stalin's part when Trotsky was released from gaol and began to overshadow him both as Chairman of the Petrograd Soviet and as a central figure in the planning and execution of the October Revolution. However, both of these roles were written out of the historical record during the period of Stalin's later ascendancy and Trotsky's political disgrace. Instead, a spurious version of the 'Great October Proletarian Socialist Revolution' was concocted which portrayed Stalin in the glorious role of Lenin's closest comrade-in-arms and veritable genius of the Revolution. On the other hand, attempts after Stalin's own death to belittle his role erred in the opposite direction. True, he kept a fairly low profile and held no operational command during the armed insurrection which overthrew the Provisional Government and declared 'All Power to the Soviets', but a recent western biographer suggests that there was really 'not a lot for him to do in the actual take-over' and that the same criticism, if criticism is called for, could be levelled at other prominent names in the party hierarchy. On the other hand, it is interesting to note that the famous eyewitness account of the Revolution written by the American journalist John Reed, *Ten Days that Shook the World*, contains not a single reference to Stalin, which no doubt accounts for the fact that the book was banned by Stalin in the 1930s and people found in possession of it were executed.

In the final analysis, it is not really important what Stalin actually did or where he actually was on the night of the insurrection. More important was the fact that despite his many years spent in the provinces, in prison or in exile, and despite his occasional differences with Lenin, he was sufficiently close to the centre of the action throughout the political turmoil of 1917, sufficiently well entrenched among the triumphant party's leading personnel, and sufficiently well experienced in organizational and ideological matters to win an automatic place as a People's Commissar (i.e. Minister) in Lenin's new revolutionary cabinet, the *Sovnarkom*. An added distinction was the fact that, of the fourteen commissariats created, Stalin's – the Commissariat for Nationalities – was the only one without a precedent in the pre-revolutionary administration of the tsars or Provisional Governments. The importance of the new office was soon to be demonstrated as the centrifugal forces of national independence threatened to dismember the fledgling revolutionary republic during the coming years of fratricidal civil war.

3

The General Secretary

Civil war

Sovnarkom's first two legislative acts were the Decree on Peace and the Decree on Land, published on 26 October 1917. Although the decrees notionally redeemed two of the Bolsheviks' revolutionary pledges – to secure peace for the country and land for the peasants – it was still the military situation and the agrarian crisis which were to prove the most intractable problems for the new regime over the next four difficult years. The most pressing task was to secure a separate peace with Germany. Trotsky, as Commissar for Foreign Affairs, was in charge of the Soviet negotiating team, but Stalin remained close to Lenin in Petrograd while the talks proceeded at Brest-Litovsk on the Russo-Polish frontier. Finally the swingeing German peace terms were agreed to, with heavy losses in territory and economic resources on the Soviet side, which caused bitter misgivings and renewed divisions within the party leadership. Although Lenin and Stalin did not always see eye-to-eye on every detail of the Brest-Litovsk treaty negotiations, nevertheless the latter ultimately supported Lenin in his pragmatic policy of 'sacrificing space in order to gain time'. Time was indeed essential, for no sooner had the Soviet government withdrawn from the international conflict than it was faced with the military resistance of its political enemies at home, supported logistically, financially, and militarily by the governments of the western capitalist powers who wished, in Winston Churchill's words, 'to strangle bolshevism in its cradle'.

This is not the place to review the course of the savage hostilities which finally led to the Red Army's victory in the Russian Civil War. Much of the credit for that victory must go to the virtual creator of the Red Army, Leon Trotsky, though one would search in vain for any such acknowledgement in later official Soviet accounts of the conflict. The conditions of warfare also gave ample scope for Stalin to demonstrate not only his organizational and administrative skills, but also those personal attributes of ruthlessness, implacability, and authoritarianism which he was to display throughout his entire career. Although he never had any soldier's training, he seemed at home in a military-style environment and was later to adopt regimental attitudes, titles, and attire. Perhaps the greatest moment of his whole career was when he led the nation to victory over Nazi Germany in 1945. He was soon after to style himself as 'Generalissimo'.

During the Civil War (1918–21) he was active on a number of different military assignments and showed great energy shuttling back and forth between Moscow (now the capital) and the different fronts – the Baltic, Byelorussia, Ukraine, Poland, and the lower Volga – where his acerbic and overweening personality often brought him into conflicts of jurisdiction and authority with local military commanders. This, however, was a common phenomenon under the system of 'dual command' introduced into the Red Army by Trotsky, whereby military commanders, often ex-tsarist officers, were 'shadowed' by a party commissar to ensure the political reliability of their orders and operations. An early and notorious example of this in Stalin's case was the 'Tsaritsyn affair' in 1918. Stalin was dispatched to the Volga town on a special mission to ensure the delivery of essential food supplies from the grain-growing areas to the north. It was essentially a civilian assignment, but Stalin soon insisted on assuming plenipotentiary military powers in the region, which brought him into collision not only with the supreme commander of the southern front, but also, more ominously for their future relations, with the People's Commissar for War, Trotsky. Eventually, some kind of compromise was found, food supplies were maintained, the local White forces retreated, and Stalin was recalled to Moscow. Some authors have maintained that the Tsaritsyn affair was a crucial element in the deadly Stalin–Trotsky rivalry of later years. Be that as it may, it certainly did nothing to sweeten their relationship, and it encouraged in Stalin his taste for power, a contempt for so-called 'experts', and an unhealthy tendency to eliminate obstacles and opponents by the use of physical force.

21

In 1920 Stalin asked to be relieved of his military duties in order to attend to the business of the Commissariat for Nationalities. The non-Russian peoples of the empire had taken advantage of the chaos of revolution and civil war in order to further their struggle for national liberation and self-determination. This was successfully achieved in the case of Finland, Poland, and the Baltic states (Estonia, Latvia, and Lithuania), but the Soviet government looked on with alarm as more and more regions and peoples from the Baltic to the Pacific sought to assert their independence from Moscow. National liberation from the Russian Empire was one thing; secession from the Soviet Socialist Republic was quite another. In this respect, therefore, the Civil War was fought in order both to achieve the political cohesiveness and to maintain the territorial integrity of the young socialist state. The Commissar for Nationalities adopted a strictly centralist stand on this issue and strove determinedly to prevent the defection of would-be secessionist states and to regather under Moscow's wing those which had managed to establish some kind of quasi-autonomy, such as the Ukraine.

In his native Transcaucasia, Stalin took a particularly hard line with the Menshevik-dominated independent government of Georgia. By 1920, neighbouring Armenia and Azerbaijan had been brought back into the Soviet fold, and in 1921, despite some initial misgivings by Lenin, the flower of Georgian independence was brutally nipped in the bud by Red Army troops. Denied even the status of a full Union Republic, the country was forcibly amalga-mated with the newly established Transcaucasian Soviet Socialist Republic and later included in the Union of Soviet Socialist Repub-lics (USSR), which was formally constituted in 1922. Not until 1936 was a semblance of statehood achieved, with the formation of the Georgian Soviet Republic.

By the time the Civil War was over Stalin had already accumulated a remarkable amount of bureaucratic power in his own hands. Despite tactical mistakes and errors of political judgement, he had made a significant contribution to the Red Army victory which greatly enhanced his personal reputation within the party (renamed the 'All-Russian Communist Party (Bolsheviks)' in 1919). Although less in the limelight than some other prominent Bolsheviks, he had managed to establish himself as a crucial cog in the government and party apparatus (*apparat*) by his willingness to undertake a whole range of essential, though unglamorous and unheroic, duties and functions which were possibly unattractive to his more sophisticated colleagues in the Kremlin leadership. Apart from the Commissariat for Nationalities, Stalin also headed the Workers' and Peasants' Inspectorate (*Rabkrin*) and was a member of the party's Organizational Bureau (*Orgburo*) and its powerful Political Bureau (*Politburo*). In April 1922 he was finally appointed to the newly created post which he was to use as the springboard for his later dictatorial power – that of General Secretary of the Communist Party. The new post was unremarkable in itself, and at the time was simply regarded as another administrative office in the party's ever-expanding bureaucratic machinery. By the time its significance was fully realized, it was too late to prevent Stalin from using it for his own ends.

NEP

The end of the Civil War did not mean that Soviet power was secure. After seven years' uninterrupted international, revolutionary, and civil warfare, Lenin's government was now beset by a wave of peasant rebellion, by military and naval mutiny, industrial chaos, depopulation, famine, international ostracism, and a desperate shortage of expert technical, cultural, and managerial manpower. In particular the economic dislocation caused by the highly centralized wartime policies known as 'War Communism' had antagonized the Russian peasantry to such an extent that Lenin was forced to reconsider his position and consolidate his power on a new foundation. In 1921 the grain-requisitioning squads of War Communism were abolished and replaced with a limited market economy in the countryside which encouraged private enterprise and profit-making in an attempt to re-harness the co-operation of the peasantry. This was the first stage of Lenin's New Economic Policy (NEP).

NEP aroused bitter controversy within the party. Although the state still controlled heavy industry and had a monopoly on foreign trade – 'the commanding heights of the economy', in Lenin's phrase – agriculture, light manufacturing, and the service industries were for the most part privately owned and managed, often by their previous owners. Many communists regarded this situation not simply as a strategic retreat from full-blown socialism and centralized planning, but at best as a compromise with capitalism and the class enemy, the bourgeoisie and the rich peasants (*kulaks*), which was insupportable during the era of what was supposed to be 'the dictatorship of the proletariat'. Lenin, however, argued that NEP was only a temporary measure, a tactical withdrawal which was essential for the stabilization of the economy, an increase in food production, and the gradual reconstruction of industry. Everyone agreed that these things were necessary for the building of socialism, especially now that proletarian revolutions had failed to materialize elsewhere in Europe, but a fierce debate raged over how the desired objective should be achieved. Nikolai Bukharin (1888–1938), one of the party's ablest theoreticians, openly called on the Russian peasants to 'Get rich', while Trotsky and the left-wing economist Pre-obrazhensky argued that the peasant must be made to pay for industrialization and socialist construction through a process of 'primary socialist accumulation', that is, squeezing capital out of the peasantry through a policy of increased taxation and agricultural pricing mechanisms. Workers' leaders complained that the initials NEP stood in reality for the 'New Exploitation of the Proletariat'.

The 'industrialization debate' was matched by another theoretical controversy over the right road to socialism, in which the two chief protagonists were Trotsky and Stalin. As early as 1906 Trotsky had formulated what came to be called his 'Theory of Permanent Re-volution', in which he argued that the weakness of the Russian bourgeoisie meant that the leading role in the bourgeois–democratic revolution would be played by the proletariat, and that this would of necessity bring about the immediate transformation of the revolu-tion into its proletarian stage and the establishment of socialism. In its turn the workers' revolution in Russia would act as the signal for a series of socialist revolutions in the advanced capitalist countries which would ensure that the Russian proletarian state would not be forced to maintain itself for long in political isolation.

Although Trotsky found many critics of his theory, including Lenin, the events of 1917 in Russia came very close to the first part of Trotsky's formulation. During the mid-twenties, however, as it became clear that the expected proletarian revolutions in the west were *not* about to take place, the question arose about the self-sufficiency of the Russian Revolution. In other words, was it possible, in the absence of world revolution, to build 'Socialism in One Country'? In a series of lectures delivered in 1924 entitled *Foundations of Leninism*, Stalin stated emphatically that the theory of permanent revolution was now untenable. Of course, he conceded, the 'final victory' of international socialism required 'the efforts of the proletarians in several advanced countries', but 'the uneven and spasmodic character of the development of the various capitalist countries . . . leads not only to the possibility, but also to the necessity of the victory of the proletariat *in individual countries'* (emphasis added). In practical political terms, Stalin's policy of constructing socialism in one country was simply more attractive to the party rank-and-file and those in the population who understood such things than the prospect held out by Trotsky and others of further revolutionary struggle. It was in a sense an appeal to nationalist instincts rather than internationalist dogma. Intellectuals in the party like Trotsky and Zinoviev, the latter chairman of the Communist International organization (*Comintern*), were easily accused of lack of faith in the Russian Revolution and of a doctrinaire refusal to believe that the Soviet Union could 'go it alone' without the support of revolutions abroad. Their objections to Socialism in One Country were, in the words of an American historian, 'ideologically impeccable and politically disastrous', particularly in the leadership struggle which followed Lenin's death in 1924.

That these economic debates and doctrinal disputes took place at all was of course a measure of the relative intellectual and political pluralism which existed during the 1920s in comparison with the rigid monolithism of the thirties. True, the country was already a one-party state and the activities of the political police (the *Cheka*) had eliminated all organized opposition to the Communists' monopoly of power. Within the party itself, the policy of 'democratic centralism' had been reinforced by the adoption of Lenin's Resolution on Party Unity at the 10th Party Congress in 1921, which outlawed the existence of organized 'factions' within the party. Nevertheless debate and discussion did take place, both inside and outside the party, with a scale and diversity that was not equalled until the late 1980s. It was a truly revolutionary, experimental era. NEP was itself an experiment, the first peacetime attempt at running a 'mixed economy' with both nationalized and private sectors peacefully coexisting. Entrepreneurship flourished. Private traders, prosperous peasants, 'bourgeois specialists' (*spetsy*), black marketeers and commodity dealers (the so-called *Nepmen*) plied their profitable businesses while the planners and politicians were locked in hot debate.

A cultural revolution, too, was taking place. Art and literature were in the avant-garde of contemporary European movements. Historians argued; critics contended; different schools of prose, poetry, and the plastic arts vied for public attention as futurism, symbolism, imaginism, constructivism, formalism, realism, and satire were challenged by the exponents of a self-consciously

25

'proletarian culture' (*Proletkult*). A whole constellation of innovative writers, artists, sculptors, dramatists, interior designers, cinematographers, and scientists combined to make the 1920s one of the most vibrant, pulsating decades in the history of Russian culture. There was, too, a genuine attempt to make all this available to the masses. This involved such initiatives as a nationwide campaign to eradicate illiteracy, progressive educational experiments, the emancipation of women, the establishment of 'workers faculties' (*rabfaks*) at the universities, the invention of new scripts for ethnic groups with no written language, and a reform of the Cyrillic alphabet which simplified orthography and facilitated the printing of books and newspapers.

To describe the 1920s as 'the halcyon days of the revolution', as one recent popular history has it, is to embroider reality. Alongside the relative freedoms and enthusiasms, the arguments and experimentation of the NEP period, there were also the evils of famine, poverty, unemployment, censorship, an oppressive bureaucracy, and all the coercive paraphernalia of the embryonic police state. But if one should not idealize the 1920s, neither should one necessarily regard them as the thin end of a Stalinist totalitarian wedge. However, as the decade drew to a close, NEP – Lenin's controversial 'compromise with capitalism' – was abandoned and Stalin began to put into drastic effect his own authoritarian version of Socialism in One Country.

Power

Before studying Stalin's 'revolution from above', it is first necessary to examine how his appointment as General Secretary in 1922 enabled him to emerge as virtual dictator in 1928. Even before Lenin's death in January 1924 the other members of the party Politburo were manoeuvring for position in the struggle for the leadership succession. In actual fact there was no formal office of 'party leader', but Lenin, who understood the realities of power politics, already realized as he lay terminally ill how the probable battle lines were being drawn. Although the Revolution had been won under the slogan of 'All Power to the Soviets', real power during the Civil War period had become more and more concentrated in the hands of the Bolshevik Party. Willy-nilly, the organs of central and local government, the soviets, had to rely to some extent on the services and expertise of functionaries and office-holders inherited from the old regime whose political reliability was naturally suspect. In response, the party began to develop its own parallel bureaucracy or *apparat* at both central and provincial levels in which full-time party officials (*cadres*) gradually dominated the administration of government as well as party policy. For the most part these new professional party bureaucrats (*apparatchiki*) were drawn from the most radical and active ranks of the working class, still fired by class hatred of the surviving representatives of the old regime, to some extent suspicious of intellectuals and 'experts', and filled with a sometimes coarse enthusiasm for the 'dictatorship of the proletariat'. However, a combination of death in war, deurbanization and dislocation of industry, unemployment, and recruitment into the party hierarchy created a situation in which, to use Isaac Deutscher's phrase, by 1921 the Bolsheviks were in the position of a 'revolutionary élite without a revolutionary class behind it'. Given the class origins of the young *apparatchiki*, the result was not so much the dictatorship of the proletariat as a 'dictatorship of some former proletarians'.

It soon became clear that the body which was in a position to dominate and control the newly emerging party bureaucracy was in a position of enormous power and influence. That body was the party Secretariat. Whoever dominated the Secretariat wielded commensurate authority. After 1922 that man was Joseph Stalin. From his office the General Secretary was able to issue administrative directives, organize agenda, make appointments, recommend promotion and dismissals, distribute personnel, and shuffle the cadres in accordance with his own preferences and ambitions. By the time Lenin died, therefore, Stalin had built up a formidable power base within the party apparatus from which he could with relative ease and on plausible pretexts conveniently isolate or neutralize those who stood in his way.

From his sick-bed, the invalided Lenin warned of the dangers of such a huge concentration of bureaucratic power in Stalin's grip. In 1922 he composed a memorandum for the guidance of the Central Committee, later known as his 'Testament', in which he evaluated the political and personal qualities of the members of the Politburo. All came in for a fair amount of criticism, but only in Stalin's case did the dying leader recommend removal from office. 'Comrade Stalin,' it read, 'having become General Secretary, has unlimited authority concentrated in his hands, and I am not sure whether he will always be capable of using that authority with sufficient caution.' A few

27

days later he added: 'Stalin is too rude, and this defect . . . is intolerable in a General Secretary. That is why I suggest that the comrades think about a way to remove Stalin from that post.' In his place they should appoint someone who is 'more tolerant, more loyal, more courteous and more considerate of the comrades, less capricious etc.' The arrogant, ill-mannered, 'nasty' side of Stalin's personality, to which there are many testimonies, fleetingly threatened his political career. However, although the details of the Testament were announced to the 1924 Party Congress, Lenin's posthumous warning was ignored and Stalin was confirmed in office by a congress that was already filled with men who owed their positions to the patronage of the General Secretary.

Stalin also survived the shifting alliances within the Politburo. At first an informal 'triumvirate' of Stalin, Zinoviev, and L. B. Kamenev (1883–1936) was formed to prevent Trotsky from taking over Lenin's mantle. The party leadership was well aware of the dangers of 'Bonapartism', that is, the emergence of a military dictator out of the flames of revolution, and Trotsky appeared to be the obvious candidate. However, by the time Zinoviev and Kamenev realized that the threat came from elsewhere, they had already compromised themselves too much to do anything effective about it. Given their previous opposition to Trotsky, the new anti-Stalin alliance of Trotsky, Zinoviev, and Kamenev was easy to denigrate as opportunist, anti-party and, following on the 1921 Resolution on Party Unity, factionalist. The penalty for factionalism was expulsion, and in 1927, during the tenth-anniversary year of the Revolution, all three Bolshevik leaders were expelled from the party. Zinoviev and Kamenev later recanted their errors and were temporarily readmitted to membership. Trotsky on the other hand was finally banished from the Soviet Union altogether in 1929, thus beginning his long decade of exile and tireless, bitter denunciations of Stalin's 'betrayal' of the Revolution.

Although intellectually Trotsky's inferior, Stalin was by far the cleverer politician. He had outmanoeuvred his arch-rival on every possible front, not least through his skilful manipulation of the 'cult' of Leninism which was established immediately after the Bolshevik leader's death and in which Stalin, the ex-seminarist, appeared in the role of high priest. In death Lenin was immortalized, almost deified, and a whole idolatrous cult built around his name, with all the ritual trappings, ceremonial, sacred texts and symbols, mythology and hagiography of a major religion. Lenin the atheist, humanist, and materialist would have turned in his grave, if he had been granted the dignity of having one. Instead his body was artificially preserved and placed on public display, where it still remains in its mausoleum today as the focal point of the nation's secular worship.

Like any self-respecting religion, the cult of Leninism also had its early heretics and apostates. Having successfully excommunicated them, Stalin now proceeded to lead the Soviet people into the promised land of Socialism in One Country. The methods he employed were to turn that country into a purgatory of human suffering and grief.

4

The totalitarian dictator

Collectivization

Although Stalin had not played a prominent role in the industrialization debate of the mid-twenties, he had never displayed particular
affection for the peasantry, and, despite personal animosities, leaned
more towards those like Trotsky who favoured a programme of
intensified industrialization at the peasants' expense. The rout of the
so-called 'Left Opposition' (Trotsky, Zinoviev, and company) in
1927 now gave Stalin a free hand to implement their economic
policies without granting them political favour. In 1928 he launched
two major initiatives which were to plunge the country into an
upheaval as great as the revolutions of 1917. These were the collectivization of agriculture and the first five-year plan for the rapid
industrialization of the economy.

Despite a fair harvest in the autumn of 1927, by the winter the
country faced an agricultural crisis. Against the background of
an international war-scare when it was widely believed that the
capitalist powers were planning another military intervention, the
peasantry began to withhold grain from the market and hoard it in
anticipation of higher prices being paid by government procurement
agencies. A number of government and party officials were dispatched to the provinces to investigate the situation. Stalin personally travelled to the Urals and western Siberia. There he solved the
problem with a characteristic lack of ceremony. Whereas other party
stalwarts still tried to reason with the peasants and operate within the

constraints of the market and NEP, Stalin simply applied force. In a reversion to the coercive tactics of War Communism, he set up road-blocks and moved in military detachments and armed requisition squads, forcing the peasants to surrender their produce under threat of criminal prosecution for 'speculation' or even grimmer consequences. It worked. As grain procurements rose in volume, Stalin determined to employ the 'Urals–Siberian method' on an even wider scale in an effort to destroy the economic power of the rich peasantry, a policy which came to be sinisterly known as 'dekulakization'. This was the beginning of a wholesome campaign of agricultural collectivization and the 'liquidation of the kulaks as a class'.

Opposition to Stalin's strong-arm methods came not just from the peasants but from within the Politburo. A so-called 'Right Opposition' led by Bukharin and the head of the government, Aleksei Rykov, objected not only to Stalin's unilateral break with Lenin's conciliatory policy of accommodating the peasants, but also to his high-handed flouting of the Politburo's collective authority. However, very much alive to the dangers of 'factionalism', the Rightists failed to organize themselves into a coherent opposition movement and found little resonance to their objections within the party *apparat* or rank-and-file. In any case the *apparat* was firmly under Stalin's control, and the short-lived Right Opposition soon followed the Left into the political wilderness.

From 1929 the collectivization drive proceeded – quite literally – in deadly earnest. The Russian countryside was once again turned into a battlefield as millions of peasant households, traditional communes, landholdings, livestock, and equipment were commandeered at gunpoint and dragooned into the huge new party-controlled collective enterprises. Kulaks were exempted. Instead, their property was confiscated and they were rounded up, herded into cattle-wagons, and forcibly transported in their millions to the frozen wastelands of Siberia and the far north where they were either left to rot or else turned into convict labourers in the work camps and industrialization projects of the five-year plan. Many resisted collectivization by burning their crops, refusing to sow, or slaughtering their herds and flocks rather than surrendering them to the collective farm (*kolkhoz*). The results, not unnaturally, were catastrophic; so much so that in the spring of 1930 Stalin called a temporary halt to the campaign. In an article entitled 'Dizzy with Success', which is breathtaking in its hypocrisy, he thundered against the misplaced

31

zealotry of local officials who in an excess of enthusiasm had rushed the process of collectivization at a breakneck speed, recklessly distorting objectives, ignoring local conditions, skipping stages, and – in a grotesque understatement – 'irritating the peasant collective farmer'!

After a temporary pause, the assault – for that is what it was – was resumed, and by 1932 over 60 per cent of all peasant households had joined the *kolkhoz*, in comparison to only around 1 per cent during the NEP. The disastrous consequences of the policy cannot be exaggerated. It yielded what has been described as a 'harvest of sorrow' for the Russian land. The collectivization drive was in effect a civil war unleashed by the party on the peasant population in which millions perished as a result of massacres, enforced deportations, and man-made famines which decimated whole provinces. In the Ukraine, a military cordon was thrown around the entire republic to prevent news of the mass starvation reaching the outside world. Only recently have the Soviet authorities begun to admit the sheer scale of the tragedy and to acknowledge that other, less brutal, less devastating options were available in order to bring about the transformation of the Soviet Union from an agrarian to a modern industrial society.

Like the rest of that society, collective farmers (*kolkhozniki*) were now mobilized to perform the bidding of the economic planners, delivering their compulsory quotas to the state at state-fixed prices, dependent on the government for mechanized equipment which was controlled through official Machine Tractor Stations (MTSs), tied to the land by a system of internal passports, and forced to respond to the dictates of party policy rather than the natural rhythms and requirements of the soil. Three-quarters of a century after the abolition of peasant bondage in Russia, the lot of the collective farmers in Stalin's USSR cannot have seemed so different from that of their enserfed forebears.

Another consequence of collectivization was the migration, part voluntary, part enforced, of nearly ten million able-bodied young peasants from the villages to join the new industrial armies of the first five-year plan.

Industrialization

In both practical and ideological terms, 'building socialism' meant economic modernization and industrialization. None of the participants in the great debates of the 1920s had disagreed on that. The arguments were over means rather than ends. Having defeated the

Left Opposition, in 1928 Stalin authorized the implementation of a complex programme setting out industrial targets for the Soviet Union's economic growth over the next quinquennium which in its scale and ambition went far beyond the projects of the most critical opponents of NEP. This was the first of the famous 'five-year plans' which have been the central feature of the Soviet 'command economy' ever since. During the period of the plan – actually concluded, if not technically completed, in four years (1929–32) – the last remaining vestiges of small-time capitalism were abolished, the *Nepmen* were eliminated, private enterprises were renationalized, and a crash programme of heavy industrial development was forced through with all the aggressive intensity and militant enthusiasm of a military campaign. Indeed, the imagery and the vocabulary of war were constantly used to describe its various features. Party propaganda trumpeted of 'industrial fronts', 'shock troops', 'storming fortresses', creating 'bastions', and of rooting out the enemy in the shape of 'spies and saboteurs'. There was, in fact, a close and conscious correlation in Stalin's mind between industrial achievement and national security, underlined by the plan's heavy emphasis on those branches of the economy which were either geared, or could be turned, to military purpose and production. Stalin made this quite explicit in a much-quoted speech of 1931 in which he blamed Russia's economic backwardness for her long record of military beatings at the hands of 'Mongol khans, . . . Turkish beys, . . . French and British capitalists . . . and Japanese barons. . . . We are fifty or a hundred years behind the advanced countries. We must make good this distance in ten. Either we do it, or they will crush us.'

To achieve this end the whole of Soviet society was mobilized and given its orders, tasks, and often unrealizable targets to fulfil. Every sector, factory, workshop, bench, and work brigade had its own allotted 'norm', its individual contribution to the plan. The whole apparatus of state control, propaganda, and coercion swung into action to inspire, exhort, or bully the nation on to ever more impossible endeavours. Huge new industrial complexes were erected in virgin territory; great dams and hydroelectric stations were built to harness the power of Russia's mighty rivers; while fuels, minerals, and raw materials were torn from the permafrost by multitudes of convict labourers toiling in the remotest regions of Siberia. Workers who overfulfilled their norm became national heroes, like Aleksei Stakhanov, the legendary miner of the mid-thirties whose name became a byword for superhuman effort. Those who underfulfilled were subject to a Draconian code of labour discipline which punished absenteeism, unpunctuality, inefficiency, and sloth. Not all the targets were reached, but underproduction was blamed on class enemies, industrial saboteurs, and the agents of foreign powers. Show trials were held of foreign experts and engineers working in Russia, accused of deliberate 'wrecking' and other criminal activities against the state and against socialism.

Despite shortfalls in certain sectors, in 1932 the plan was declared to have been fulfilled. A tremendous leap forward had been made in industrial output, particularly in the metallurgical industries. Socialist planning methods appeared to have been vindicated at a time when western capitalism seemed to be in ruins, racked by mass unemployment and economic depression. In material terms the achievements and triumphs of the early five-year plans were truly heroic. It is impossible to put even approximate figures on production levels, as the official statistics were, to say the least, untrustworthy, but there was no denying that the foundations had been well and truly laid for the transformation of the USSR into an industrial giant. In human terms, however, the cost of this industrial progress was staggering. Machinery and equipment had at first to be bought from abroad, purchased with the revenue from exports of grain screwed from the collective farmers while the people starved. Food and consumer goods disappeared from the shops; interminable queuing became a regular feature of daily existence; rationing was introduced; housing conditions in the overcrowded cities were appalling; wages failed to keep pace with rocketing prices. Under socialism, Stalin assured the Soviet people, 'life is getting better, more joyful'.

Life was certainly getting different. The economic transformation brought about by collectivization and industrialization was accompanied by a social and cultural revolution. Soviet society now consisted officially of two classes, the workers and the *kolkhozniki*, and a social 'stratum' of educated white-collar workers and professional personnel known as the 'intelligentsia'. Everyone, not just workers and peasants, had their part to play in the plan. Creative writers were to be, in Stalin's phrase, 'engineers of human souls' and a new literary/political formula called 'Socialist Realism' was introduced as a yardstick against which all kinds of artistic endeavour were to be measured. Censorship controls were reinforced to ensure that authors wrote in such a way as to enhance and glorify the victory of socialism. Gone were the independent literary groupings of the 1920s, replaced in 1934 by the Union of Soviet Writers, a kind of literary closed shop whose members assembled novels and stories full of compulsory optimism and positive heroes. Lyricism, romance, formalism, and satire were taboo. Instead, the state-owned printing presses churned out the monochrome conveyor-belt novels of the five-year plan with stirring titles such as Ostrovsky's *How the Steel was Tempered* (1935) and Gladkov's *Cement* (1934).

Not only literature, but all other forms of artistic, intellectual, and even scientific activity were subject to ideological requirements. Stalin himself became the final arbiter on every academic discipline from agronomy to zoology. Biologists, geneticists, lawyers, linguists, and musicians were forced to toe the party line. History became the handmaiden of the state. The great figures of Russia's past, temporarily debunked by the Marxist historiography of the twenties, were rehabilitated. Strong rulers like Ivan the Terrible and Peter the Great, military leaders like Generals Suvorov and Kutuzov, were now depicted as national heroes. The analogy with the wise and omnipotent Stalin was deliberate and unmistakable. On the other hand heroes of the revolutionary struggle of 1917, Trotsky in particular, were ignominiously 'unpersoned' and cast into historical limbo.

As the thirties wore on, other remnants of the past were revived in an attempt to replace the libertarianism of the revolutionary period with more order, discipline, and control. Educational experiments were scrapped and schools made to reintroduce learning by rote, formal examinations, a core curriculum, and school uniforms. In personal relationships, cohabitation, easy divorce, and abortion on demand were all but abolished as the virtues of the stable nuclear family, fecundity, and parenthood were stressed. 'Mother-heroines' who produced ten children or more were awarded medals by the grateful state, a reflection, perhaps, of the five-year plan's emphasis on quantitative achievement. In the armed services, there was a return to the use of tsarist ranks and titles for the officer class, together with more elaborate uniforms, insignia, and regalia. In civil society the concept of 'dangerous egalitarianism' was officially condemned and a whole range of wage and salary differentials, perks and privileges, special shops and exclusive honours introduced for members of what Djilas called 'the new class' of party bosses and the bureaucratic establishment. Stalin's revolution from above had abandoned the pristine revolutionary slogans of 'Liberty,

Equality, Fraternity' in favour of oppression, inequality, and strife.

In 1934 the Party celebrated its successes at the 17th Congress – triumphantly entitled the 'Congress of Victors'. The worst excesses of collectivization and the first five-year plan were at an end; socialism had been achieved and the old class enemies defeated; the second five-year plan promised more to the consumer; old oppositionists had been readmitted to the party fold; soon a new constitution was to be drafted which was hailed as 'the most democratic in the world'. There was a sense of accomplishment and a mood of self-congratulation. The worst, it seemed, was over. But the worst was yet to come.

Terror

Just at the time when his power seemed more secure, when the party seemed united, when the industrial and agricultural economy were showing results and the sacrifices of the recent past seemed justified, Stalin plunged the entire country into a paroxysm of pain and sheer terror which many believe to be unprecedented in human history.

The first target of his attack was the party itself, and the first victim was the popular leader of the Leningrad party organization, Sergei Kirov (1886–1934). Kirov was shot at his headquarters on 1 December 1934 by an ex-member of the Communist Youth Organization named Leonid Nikolayev. Although it has never been definitely proven, there is much circumstantial evidence to suggest that the instigator of the assassination was Stalin himself. There were those in the party who favoured Kirov as a possible alternative to Stalin as General Secretary, though it is highly unlikely that Kirov was himself involved in any specific challenge or plot. Whatever the exact circumstances – and they may never be known – Stalin used Kirov's murder as the pretext for the immediate introduction of a series of extraordinary anti-terrorist measures and an extensive purge of those suspected of complicity in the affair. The most prominent of the arrested suspects were former Politburo members, Kamenev and Zinoviev. In January 1935 they were tried and sentenced to imprisonment for allegedly maintaining a terrorist 'Centre' in Moscow and exercising ideological influence over Kirov's assassin. Other, less prominent suspects were summarily executed by the secret police, the NKVD (People's Commissariat for Internal Affairs). This was the beginning of the sinister process of political and physical

36

blood-letting over the next four years often referred to as 'The Great Terror'.

The public manifestation of this Soviet holocaust was the notorious show trials staged in Moscow between 1936 and 1938. At the first, in August 1936, Zinoviev, Kamenev, and others were hauled from their cells to confess to a catalogue of crimes against the people, including plotting with the exiled Trotsky to murder Stalin and other members of the Politburo. There was no material evidence brought against them and no defence. The accused confessed their guilt and were immediately shot. During their confessions from the dock they had implicated others in their crimes, including Bukharin and members of the Right Opposition. Their arrest and trial was only a matter of time.

At the second major trial, in 1937, other once-respected old Bolsheviks confessed to similar charges and met a similar fate. Finally, in March 1938, 'the trial of the 21' took place at which Bukharin, Rykov, and former NKVD chief Genrikh Yagoda (1891–1938) – who had earlier set up the trial of Zinoviev and Kamenev! – faced the state prosecutor, the odious ex-Menshevik Andrei Vyshinsky (1885–1954). In addition to the 'normal' charges of maintaining links with Trotsky, plotting murder, and industrial sabotage, Bukharin and company were accused of conspiring with foreign intelligence agencies to sell out parts of the Soviet Union to imperialist Japan and Nazi Germany. Bukharin actually dared to deny some of the charges in detail, but his general confession was sufficient to earn him the NKVD's by now routine bullet in the back of the skull. In the words of the official history of the Communist Party, published in 1939:

These contemptible lackeys of the fascists forgot that the Soviet people had only to move a finger, and not a trace of them would be left.
The Soviet court sentenced the Bukharin–Trotsky fiends to be shot.
The People's Commissariat of Internal Affairs carried out the sentence.
The Soviet people approved the annihilation of the Bukharin–Trotsky gang and moved on to next business.

The Moscow trials were merely the tip of a huge iceberg the dimensions of which can only be guessed at. Only those who the security forces, the NKVD interrogators, and the public prosecutor

37

knew would confess in open court, would play their part, and repeat their lines in this macabre masquerade of justice actually made it to the dock. Otherwise the show would flop.

Behind the scenes the agents of the NKVD conducted a huge drag-net operation, scouring the country for all known and suspected associates, colleagues, relatives, and acquaintances of the central characters. In the interrogation chambers of the Lubyanka prison in Moscow and in police cells throughout Russia, tens, hundreds of thousands of bewildered, frightened citizens, loyal communists, dedicated revolutionaries, and party functionaries found themselves victims of the dreaded pre-dawn knock and their anonymous accusers. The memoirs of those who survived make harrowing reading. Sophisticated interrogation techniques, physical and mental torture, deprivation of sleep, threats to close relatives, and the administration of narcotic drugs were used with deadly finesse in order to weed out and destroy the 'enemies of the people'. The concepts of guilt by association, guilt by category, guilt by occupation, guilt by admission, and guilt by silence were introduced as a means of widening the murderous trawl. Many foreign comrades, having fled to the bastion of socialism from their persecutors in fascist Europe, now sat and pondered the cruel irony of their fate in Stalin's dungeons.

The shock-waves soon reverberated far beyond the party *apparat*. Government officials, members of the diplomatic corps, leaders of national minorities, teachers of foreign languages, journalists, and leading academics suffered in the onslaught on the intelligentsia. In 1938 the Red Army was literally decapitated by a military purge which swept away almost all its senior staff and commanding officers on the eve of a major war (much, incidentally, to Hitler's satisfaction). Not even the internal security services themselves were immune. Yagoda, author of the first purge trial, was arrested and replaced as head of the NKVD by Nikolai Yezhov (1895–1939?), 'the bloodthirsty dwarf', whose name has become synonymous with the terror, still known in Russian as the *Yezhovshchina*. Ultimately, Yezhov himself was sacked and his place taken by the no less repulsive Lavrenty Beria (1899–1953), Stalin's fellow Georgian, who was given the task of 'purging the purgers', a job he undertook with lethal relish. Yezhov himself disappeared, probably shot.

It is now traditional to note at this stage that the final victim of the Great Terror was Leon Trotsky, murdered in 1940 in far-off Mexico when one of Stalin's agents buried an ice-pick in his brain.

38

The terror of the 1930s was of course a nightmare phenomenon which nevertheless actually happened. And, like all nightmares, its reasons and its meaning are difficult to unravel. For millions of its victims it meant, of course, imprisonment, torture, execution, or the living death of exile in the charnel-house of Stalin's concentration camps, damningly immortalized in Alexander Solzhenitsyn's work as *The Gulag Archipelago* (*GULag* is the Russian abbreviation for the Main Prison Camp Administration). The stark horror of the camps is captured in their description by one of the survivors as 'Auschwitz without the ovens'. For the party the terror meant almost a complete change of personnel, the physical destruction of the old Bolsheviks and their replacement by a whole new generation of reliable, unquestioning, and unimaginative sycophants who owed their lives and their careers to their willingness to step into dead men's shoes. They were a different breed of Communists, creatures of Stalin who had been unnaturally selected through a process which ensured the survival of the dullest. It meant the emasculation of the intelligentsia and the rape of Soviet science and culture. For many national minorities it meant mass deportation from their traditional homelands. For Stalin himself it meant the extermination of his rivals and critics – past and potential, real and imagined – and the ultimate consolidation of his tyrannical power. And for the Soviet people it meant almost half a century of fear, suspicion, ignorance of their own past and the outside world, and a fatalistic submissiveness to the totalitarian system he created.

To seek rational explanations for such an irrational and complex phenomenon as the Great Terror is an impossible task. Some writers regard Stalin's blood purge as the logical and unavoidable consequence of original Bolshevik theory and practice. In this view, Lenin's advocacy of an elite, highly centralized and disciplined party must inevitably give rise to the tyranny of a single dictator. However, although Lenin was not personally squeamish in his methods of dealing with opposition, there is nothing in the body of his writings or in his own political behaviour which authorizes, condones, or envisages the systematic slaughter of several million guiltless citizens. Others have suggested that the premature nature of the Russian Revolution, which sought to create a highly industrialized socialist society in a backward, peasant country, necessarily involved the use of force on a massive scale in order to achieve the Revolution's objectives. Again, there is a qualitative difference between the use of violence in a revolutionary situation and the cold-blooded deliberate annihilation of whole sections of the population. Many have pointed to the exigencies of the international situation in the 1930s: in order to preserve the territorial and political integrity of the USSR against the threat of European fascism and Nazism, it was essential to ensure that internally the country remained strongly united and that all potential sources of political opposition which might have weakened the Soviet system from within be eliminated at all costs. The victory of the Red Army over the Germans at the battle of Stalingrad in 1943 – so runs this argument – proved that Stalin's policies were right. On the other hand it has been fairly objected that, 'but for Stalin's policies, the Germans would not have got as far as Stalingrad'! Indeed, one might go further to suggest that, but for Stalin's policies, the Germans might never have dared to cross the Soviet frontier in the first place.

Then there is the psychological interpretation which attributes Stalin's terror simply to the paranoid machinations of a criminally deranged psycopath, of a morbidly suspicious and vindictive megalomaniac suffering from the combination of an inferiority complex and delusions of grandeur mixed with homicidal tendencies. Clearly, his behaviour was far from normal, but the present author – like many of those who *have* confidently offered such a diagnosis – is not medically qualified to give an authoritative opinion on the clinical aspects of the case. Recently a hypothesis has been put forward which suggests that the purges should be seen as a natural disaster like a flood or tempest which periodically sweeps through a land, ravaging the population and destroying everything in its path. Unlike the forces of nature, however, the causes of human tragedies must be sought in the activities of human beings. Unfortunately, none of the explanations of the Great Terror so far advanced by historians, political scientists, or psychoanalysts may be regarded as wholly safe or satisfactory.

In 1939, the purges were declared to be over. In the same year Stalin's Commissar for Foreign Affairs, Vyacheslav Molotov (1890 –1986), signed a treaty of mutual non-aggression with his German opposite number, von Ribbentrop. While Europe was at war, the infamous *Pakt* was to buy the Soviet Union two years of relative peace before she was hurled into yet another nightmare of horror and unimaginable suffering in the shape of the Nazi invasion under the code-name 'Barbarossa'.

5

The military leader

Barbarossa

Very little has so far been said about Stalin's conduct of foreign policy. During the 1920s the Soviet Union pursued an ambiguous and seemingly contradictory course in its relations with the outside world. On the one hand she needed to establish a peaceful working relationship with the hostile capitalist powers with which she was surrounded, if possible gaining diplomatic recognition and establishing overseas trade links. On the other hand, the government was still ideologically committed to the concept of world revolution and the overthrow of the capitalist system with which it was, nevertheless, striving peacefully to coexist. To this end, Lenin had inaugurated the Third (Communist) International (*Comintern*) in March 1919. However, it soon became apparent that, as in its dealings with foreign governments, so with foreign communist parties, the immediate national self-interest of the Soviet Union was paramount and took precedence over the long-term ideological goal of international communism. Lenin's disputes with the so-called Left Communists over the treaty of Brest-Litovsk established the precedent, and Stalin was later to reinforce the primacy of nationalist over internationalist aims with his policy of Socialism in One Country, even if this meant abandoning foreign comrades in favour of alliances with moderate political parties. In China, this policy ended in tragedy in 1927 when the Comintern-backed nationalist

41

forces of Chiang Kai-shek's Kuomintang slaughtered the Chinese communists in Shanghai.

In Europe, Stalin's policy towards the German Communist Party can be seen in retrospect to have been equally tragic, though for different reasons and with more calamitous repercussions for the security of the Soviet Union. In close step with his 1928 left wheel in domestic policies, through the Comintern Stalin ordered that there should be no political or electoral alliance between communist and other left-wing or socialist parties. The German Social Democrats were smeared with political abuse as 'social fascists' even when the example of Mussolini's Italy had already given warning of the danger from the extreme right, and when the German National Socialist (*Nazi*) Party was gaining strength in the dying days of the Weimar Republic. While not itself directly responsible, this ultra-sectarian policy towards the left arguably facilitated the electoral victory of Adolf Hitler (1889–1945) as German Chancellor in 1933. But still Stalin underestimated the menace of fascism and Nazism, and continued with his vilification of Europe's non-communist left.

In 1935 the seventh congress of the Third International convened in Moscow, at which Stalin unashamedly announced a U-turn in Comintern policy. Hitler's aggressive domestic and foreign policies had finally persuaded Stalin where the real danger lay and prompted him to order the formation of 'popular fronts' of all parties of the left, centre, and even moderate right in order to combat the evils of fascism and National Socialism in Europe. In his speeches Hitler had made no secret of his racialist contempt for the Slavs as well as his political hatred of bolshevism; nor did he conceal his territorial ambitions in the east, where the Soviet Ukraine would provide ample 'living space' (*Lebensraum*) for the master race of conquering Aryans. Against this threat, Stalin sought the collective security of an alliance with the European democracies, which seemed, however, more intent on appeasing Hitler's militant ambitions and standing meekly by – or, indeed, actively collaborating – as the Führer steadily expanded the power of the Third Reich.

The remilitarization of the Rhineland, the anti-Comintern pact of Germany, Italy, and Japan, the annexation of Austria, and German–Italian aid to Franco's rebel forces during the Spanish Civil War were sufficient examples of Hitler's aggressive intentions and his deter-mination to put them into effect. Simultaneous confrontation with imperial Japan in the Far East faced the Soviet Union with the possibility of having to fight a war on two fronts and Stalin with the problem of how to avoid it. In 1938 Russia was deliberately excluded from the negotiations in Munich which led to Hitler's dismemberment of Czechoslovakia. Stalin now had to think hard. The western powers had more or less abandoned republican Spain to its fate. Independent Czechoslovakia had been sacrificed on the altar of appeasement. The Red Army high command had been nearly annihilated in Stalin's purge. Soviet troops were already fighting the Japanese at the battles of Lake Khasan and Khalkhin-Gol. What guarantee was there that a formal military alliance against Hitler would bring Britain and France speeding to Moscow's aid in case of a German attack? Unfortunately, there were many circles in Europe who thought that this would be no bad thing. Procrastination and lack of purpose marked the French and British responses to Russia's offer of a Franco-British-Soviet anti-Nazi alliance. Finally Stalin did the unthinkable. He concluded a pact with Hitler.

Looked at in terms of *Realpolitik* and the Soviet Union's own security, the Nazi-Soviet treaty of non-aggression was a sensible move. Morally and politically it outraged the European left and tore the 'popular front' to shreds. Militarily, it gave Hitler a free hand to launch the invasion of Poland. Britain and France declared war on Germany but initially took no direct action to rescue Poland. However, the Second World War had now begun.*

The *Pakt* did not make the Soviet Union and Nazi Germany allies. It simply guaranteed their mutual non-aggression. It also incidentally allowed Stalin to occupy parts of eastern Poland and reincorporate the Baltic republics of Estonia, Latvia, and Lithuania into the Soviet Union. This was carried out with great brutality during 1939–40 and involved the enforced 'sovietization' of all public and private institutions and the mass deportation of thousands of Balts and Poles to Siberia and Central Asia. (Over 14,000 Polish army officers were massacred and buried in mass graves at Katyn in Byelorussia, an atrocity which was almost certainly carried out by Soviet security forces.) The ostensible reason for all this activity was the strengthening of the Soviet Union's western defences, a policy which was further pursued during the 'Winter War' of 1939–40 against Finland. The courageous Finns put up a bitter and sustained resistance but were eventually forced to cede considerable territory to the Soviet invaders.

*Ruth Henig, *The Origins of the Second World War 1933–1939*, Lancaster Pamphlets, Methuen, London, 1985.

For almost two years after the *Pakt* was signed, anti-Nazi propaganda was played down in the Soviet Union, Russo-German commercial and diplomatic relations continued, and the country was lulled into a false sense of security. However, having made himself master of continental Europe, Hitler once more turned his thoughts towards the east. It is clear that plans to attack the Soviet Union were being laid soon after the fall of France in June 1940, but Stalin unaccountably refused to heed the warnings of reliable intelligence sources concerning Hitler's intentions. German troop and naval deployments, information from espionage circles in occupied Europe, from defecting German soldiers, from Winston Churchill, from the Soviet master-spy Richard Sorge in Tokyo – Stalin chose to ignore them all, and dismissed as 'provocative' the advice of his senior military officers to mobilize.

At 0415 on Sunday 22 June 1941 Hitler struck. The German armies invaded on a broad front with a three-pronged lightning assault (*Blitzkrieg*) aimed at Leningrad in the north, Moscow in the centre, and Kiev and the Ukraine to the south. As their tanks raced virtually unopposed across Soviet territory, *Luftwaffe* bombs demolished the Soviet airforce before its planes could leave the ground. The onslaught took the Russian people completely by surprise. Army command was paralysed through lack of orders. Stalin was stunned. Operation Barbarossa – 'the biggest military operation ever mounted' – was under way.

Stalingrad

This is not the place to give a blow-by-blow account of the Nazi–Soviet conflict. Some details are, however, necessary. By the early autumn the country was in a totally demoralized state. The *Wehrmacht* had penetrated swiftly and deeply into Soviet territory. The whole of Byelorussia and parts of the Ukraine were in enemy hands. Millions of prisoners were taken. Leningrad was besieged and in the grip of a murderous blockade during which over a million of its citizens were to perish in horrifying conditions – more than the total combined British and American casualties in the entire war. One after another, major Soviet cities fell – Minsk, Smolensk, Riga, Tallin, Pskov, Kiev, Kharkov, Odessa – until by mid-October German troops were in the outskirts of Moscow, only a few kilometres from the Kremlin.

The astonishing speed of the German advance was facilitated by a

44

number of factors: the surprise of the attack and the unpreparedness of the Soviet forces; Stalin's obstinacy in refusing to believe it was imminent; the superior equipment and armour of the German troops; the low morale of the population, which had barely recovered from the rigours of collectivization, the five-year plans, and the purge (in some areas the Germans were initially greeted as liberators); and finally the poor quality and inexperience of the officer corps – a direct result of the recent purge of the military. Nor did the 'scorched earth' policy carried out by the retreating Russian soldiers create a major obstacle. On 3 July Stalin addressed the nation with a speech in which he called for the destruction of everything which might be of use to the invader:

> the enemy must not be left a single engine, a single railway truck, not a single pound of grain or gallon of fuel . . . In occupied areas, partisan units must be formed, sabotage groups must be formed . . . to blow up bridges and roads, damage telephone and telegraph wires, set fire to forests, stores and transport . . . conditions must be made intolerable for the enemy and all his accomplices.

Where there was time, factories, plant, machinery, and their workforces were uprooted and shipped eastwards to be relocated in the hinterland beyond the Urals. As if in replication of Lenin's policy at Brest-Litovsk, Stalin was in effect sacrificing space in order to buy time: time to recover from the shock of invasion, to regather the country's strength, to work out strategy, to gear the whole nation – man, woman, and child – to the war effort, and time to carry out delicate diplomatic manoeuvres with the Soviet Union's new, unlikely, allies, first Britain and then the United States.

The battle for Moscow was launched in October and raged throughout November and the first days of December. The German forces were over-extended and ill equipped to deal with the rigours of a particularly atrocious Russian winter. Warm clothing was in short supply; fuel froze in its tanks; leather German jackboots cracked apart and thousands died of frostbite as Marshal Zhukov, commander of the western front, launched a savage counter-offensive, reinforced by snow-toughened Siberian troops fresh from the Far Eastern front. Moscow was saved. The Germans fell back 150 kilometres and Stalin reaped the glory.

The defence of Moscow, which Stalin never left, was a tremendous morale-booster for the Soviet people as a whole and for Stalin in particular. The whole country was united as it had not been united since before the Revolution. A superhuman effort was made to increase armaments production and reconstitute industrial war losses. Old enemies were rehabilitated and released from the camps. Even the Russian Orthodox Church was later restored to favour as a reward for its patriotic efforts and appeals for the defence of 'Holy Russia'. The victories of past heroes like Prince Alexander Nevsky, Dmitry Donskoy, Minin and Pozharsky, and General Kutuzov were celebrated in official propaganda and constant analogies drawn between Hitler's invasion and Napoleon's ill-fated campaign of 1812. Tolstoy's great novel *War and Peace* was reprinted in thousands of cheap editions to remind people of their former triumph. The whole of Russian society, soldier and factory hand, peasant and party official, stood shoulder-to-shoulder to defend Russia in what is still referred to as the 'Great Patriotic War'.

Paradoxically, perhaps, wartime saw a number of further relaxations in official policy. Restrictions on party membership were loosened as millions of new members hurried to join its ranks; literature flourished as authors filled their books with epics of patriotic endeavour; the Comintern was disbanded in deference to the new alliance with the western democracies; and in its propaganda the government toned down the ideological antagonism between socialism and capitalism, calling on the allies to defend democracy against fascism. Not that propaganda was necessary to stir up patriotic enthusiasm; the barbaric, racially inspired treatment of the civilian population by the invaders was more than sufficient to inflame anti-German hatred to fever pitch. Villages were razed to the ground, women and children raped and tortured, Jews, communists, and ordinary Russians systematically butchered as Hitler's agents carried out his genocidal policies which officially cast the Slavs as 'subhuman' (*Untermenschen*), fit only for slavery or slaughter.

To their cost, the German armies were soon to discover the almost superhuman, fanatical fighting qualities of the Russian soldier in the battle which was to become the decisive turning-point in the war. Having failed to take Moscow, and with Leningrad still suffering the horrors of the continuing siege, Hitler concentrated his attentions on the southern front. The whole of the Ukraine was overrun and for a moment it looked as if the Caucasus would suffer a similar fate. However, Hitler made the fatal decision to throw his armies at the city on the Volga which bore Stalin's name – Stalingrad. Tactically speaking, Stalingrad (the old Tsaritsyn) was not a vital objective, but

Hitler seemed to be hypnotized by the prospect of destroying 'Stalin's city'. By August 1942 his troops were in the suburbs, encircling the town and squeezing the Soviet 62nd Army with its back to the river. Throughout the autumn and winter of 1942–3 the greatest and fiercest battle of the Second World War was fought in the streets and houses of a single town. For Stalin and for the entire nation Stalingrad epitomized the burden of the war which the Soviet Union felt it was bearing single-handed. Certainly the western allies' failure to open up the promised second front in Europe in 1942 meant that Hitler could concentrate his attention on the east, forcing Russia to bear the brunt of the hostilities for another two years.

It is impossible to convey the horror and the heroism, the courage and the carnage of Stalingrad in so little space. Street-to-street, room-to-room, and hand-to-hand combat raged with a savage intensity in which, to quote Isaac Deutscher, 'the conquest of a single street cost the Germans as much time and blood as they had hitherto spent on the conquest of entire European countries'. Hitler fulminated that there should be no retreat. Stalin issued his famous command, 'Not one step back!' Gradually the dogged Russian resistance turned into a fierce counter-offensive. General von Paulus's 6th Army was surrounded by a Soviet pincer movement and cut off from its Italian and Romanian reinforcements to the west. Hitler insisted frantically on no surrender, but finally the exhausted, decimated Germans were forced into submission. Von Paulus capitulated on 2 February 1943. With him twenty-four generals and nearly 100,000 men were captured, leaving another 70,000 German dead in the ruins of Stalingrad.

Stalin was triumphant. In March he assumed the rank of Marshal of the Soviet Union and later Churchill presented him with a ceremonial sword from the British monarch, King George VI, as a mark of his personal esteem for the Soviet feat of arms. The victory on the Volga had shown that the *Wehrmacht* was no longer invincible. The tide of war had changed.

Victory

The battle was won but another two years of devastating warfare were to follow before the occupied areas were liberated and Nazi Germany defeated. Stalingrad was a crushing personal blow for Hitler. His mental and psychological deterioration after the defeat seemed to be matched by the slow, inexorable collapse of his eastern front as the Red Army drove relentlessly westwards. But the German army was still a formidable opponent and many major battles remained to be fought, including the battle for Kursk in July 1943 which turned out to be the biggest tank battle of the Second World War. The roll-call of cities which had fallen to the Germans in 1941–2 was now put into reverse as the Ukraine and Byelorussia were gradually liberated during 1943 and 1944. In the north the siege of Leningrad was finally lifted early in 1944, and by the summer Soviet troops were pushing into Poland and the Balkans with the Germans in full retreat well before the allied landings in Normandy finally opened the second front. In May 1945 Red Army troops under the command of Marshal Zhukov entered the German capital and planted the red flag on top of the Berlin Reichstag. The formal German surrender to the victorious allies was signed at Soviet army headquarters in Berlin on 8 May 1945 (9 May, Moscow time). The war in Europe was over.

Stalin was at the height of his power and popularity both at home and abroad. In June 1945 he adopted the title of 'Generalissimo' and was universally acknowledged as one of the great wartime leaders. In the closing stages of the war he had met on equal terms with the British Prime Minister, Churchill, and the American President, Roosevelt, at the allied conferences in Teheran (1943), Yalta, and Potsdam (1945) at which the political boundaries of post-war Europe were drawn. During the negotiations, which Churchill was later to describe as a process of 'horse-trading', continental Europe was divided into respective 'zones' or 'spheres of influence' between the Soviet Union and the western powers. Germany itself, including Berlin, was carved up into British, American, French, and Soviet sectors, while the overwhelming Red Army presence in eastern and south-eastern Europe guaranteed that these countries would remain firmly under Stalin's sway. Before the war the Soviet Union had been politically isolated, surrounded by the hostile 'capitalist encirclement' and intent on building Socialism in One Country. Stalin now bestrode half of a prostrate Europe and the Soviet Union was poised to emerge as one of the world's two military and political 'superpowers' which were soon to confront each other during the tense years of the 'Cold War'.

However, the flush of victory and the territorial and diplomatic gains in eastern Europe could do little to solace the country's battered population, or what was left of it. From Russia's point of view, the war was probably the greatest Pyrrhic victory in history. Twenty

million of the Soviet population – one in [...]
half of them civilians and the majority of t[...]
age-group. The resulting sexual imbalance and [...]
sequences were to last for many years to come[...]
survived, hundreds of thousands were left crippled, [...]
unfit for work. Apart from the physical mutilations, whol[...]
of Soviet citizens were left psychologically scarred for life. In [...]
the shocking slaughter left a deep and ineradicable trauma in t[...]
mind and soul of the Soviet people which has only quite recently
begun to heal, though the visible and invisible scars still remain. The
sheer scale of the human suffering and material destruction is
unimaginable. Complete cities, towns, villages, and settlements
were obliterated, leaving around twenty-five million homeless. In
Stalingrad, 90 per cent of the city was flattened. In Leningrad, more
people died through shelling, cold, or starvation than were killed by
the American atomic bombs dropped on Hiroshima and Nagasaki.
To anyone visiting the Piskarevskoye memorial cemetery in
Leningrad today the agony and the grief are almost tangible, as if
congealed in the very atmosphere.

The victory was therefore bought at a terrible price, not only for
the fighting men but also for the civilian population. Peace, however, brought only the briefest respite. As Stalin consolidated his
grip on the countries of eastern Europe and as the uneasy warmth of
the Grand Alliance began to freeze and harden into the enmity of the
Cold War, the long-suffering Soviet people now faced the Herculean
task of national reconstruction.

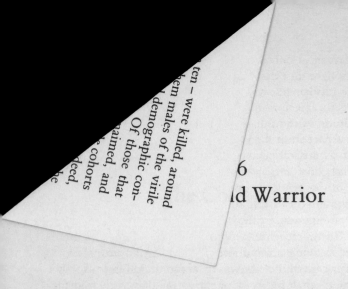

Reconstruction

A physically debilitated and emotionally distraught nation was now called upon to restore its shattered economy. Over one-quarter of the industrial capacity of the Soviet Union had been destroyed, and in those areas occupied by the enemy the proportion was even higher, around 65 per cent. In particular the heavy industries such as iron, steel, and fuel, which had been given special emphasis during the five-year plans, were badly hit. Hundreds of factories, foundries, mines, and workshops had been either devastated in the fighting or demolished by the scorched-earth policies of the retreating armies, both Russian and German. What could be saved had been transported east and relocated in a desperate programme of territorial diversification of industry which successfully enhanced production levels after the initial onslaught.

Light industry had also suffered. During the war years all industry was geared to military or paramilitary output with little or no spare capacity for consumer-goods production. This had, of course, been a feature of the pre-war economic priorities and the same pattern was now to be repeated in the new five-year plan for national reconstruction (1946–50), with a consequent continuation of material hardship, shortages of essential goods, and a depressed standard of living for the foreseeable future. The situation was exacerbated by the low priority given to the construction of domestic accommodation in favour of capital building and rebuilding projects and it was not until well into the 1950s that large-scale housing schemes got under way to alleviate the desperate shortage. Transport and communication networks had likewise been ruined and strenuous efforts had to be made to replace railways, rolling stock, and blown-up bridges. Agriculture was in a shambles. In the occupied areas where farms had been decollectivized, a crash programme of recollectivization was instituted, but a combination of lack of manpower on the land, shortage of livestock and machinery, drought, and dubious planning methods ensured that agriculture long remained the Achilles' heel of the Soviet economy.

Despite the hardships and the sacrifices, progress was made. Some of the industrial losses were made good by the import of capital equipment from the defeated countries, in particular the Soviet sector of Germany, in the shape of reparations and war booty. Shortfalls in manpower were to some extent offset by utilizing the forced labour of prisoners of war, around two million of whom were detained in Soviet labour camps until long after the end of the war. Even Soviet POWs returning home from captivity in Europe now found themselves once more behind barbed wire as Stalin punished them for having surrendered or succumbed to the enemy! The technological expertise of captured or commandeered foreign specialists and scientists was also made to contribute to the nation's recovery. They also assisted in the race to match the United States' recently demonstrated nuclear capability. But the major contribution to national revival was made by the spectacular exertions of the Soviet working population, which was called upon yet again to conquer almost insurmountable obstacles in what were still generally appalling conditions. Genuine enthusiasm to make good the war losses was reinforced by a return to the strict communal discipline and Draconian methods of the 1930s. Stalin abandoned the relative relaxations of the war years and marshalled all the resources of the police state to reimpose the controls of his totalitarian system with a renewed vigour.

The cult of Stalin himself, already well established in the 1930s but now illuminated by the aureole of martial glory, assumed new dimensions. Extravagant, incredible, even ludicrous claims were made concerning his revolutionary zeal, his intellectual prowess, his economic achievements, his military leadership, and his omniscient wisdom. Stalin was hailed as the Father of the Peoples, the Captain of Industry, the Closest Comrade-in-Arms of Lenin, the Great Educator, the Mighty Leader, even the Shining Sun! The panegyrics knew no bounds. This was not just hero-worship; this was deification.

No one dared query Stalin's word. Even his servile creatures on the party Politburo were, in Nikita Khrushchev's chilling phrase, only 'temporary people' who never knew on leaving Stalin's presence whether they would end up at home in bed or in the cells of the Lubyanka. At one of his increasingly frequent drinking bouts, Stalin once ordered the portly Khrushchev to dance the Ukrainian *Gopak*, squatting on his haunches and kicking out his heels. Khrushchev painfully but prudently obeyed. As he later observed to his fellow Politburo member Anastas Mikoyan, 'When Stalin says "Dance", a wise man dances.'

Outside the closed circle of his political minions, the rest of the population also danced to Stalin's bidding. Apart from the toiling peasants and workers, members of the artistic and scientific intelligentsia were all compelled to perform according to the dictates of the master choreographer. One of the most serious casualties was the science of genetics, which was set back a whole generation because of Stalin's support for the ideologically convenient but scientifically spurious theories of the bogus biologist Lysenko, who claimed that acquired characteristics could be genetically transmitted. Only maths and physics seemed to be safe from interference, no doubt because of their strategic and military applications.

In the humanities, linguistics, philosophy, and even music were forced into the Stalinist straitjacket, but it was literature which bore the brunt of Stalin's renewed attack on creative freedom. The 'Great Educator's' chief hatchet-man in the artistic slaughterhouse of the late 1940s was Andrei Zhdanov (1896–1948), the man who had succeeded the murdered Kirov as boss of the Leningrad party organization in 1934. In 1946 the so-called 'Zhdanov decrees' were promulgated, which introduced a period of such cultural sterility and talentless uniformity as to outrival even the 'socialist realist' mediocrities of the 1930s. After closing down two Leningrad journals for publishing material which allegedly 'kowtowed' to western literary fashion, Zhdanov singled out two writers for especially vicious abuse and public humiliation, Mikhail Zoshchenko, a writer of satirical short stories, and the popular lyric poetess and veteran of the Leningrad siege, Anna Akhmatova. The intensely personal love themes and religious imagery of much of Akhmatova's verse led Zhdanov to pillory her as 'part nun, part whore' who divided her time between the convent and the brothel. The crude invective apart, the extreme nationalism with which Zhdanov's campaign was suffused was not without its anti-Semitic overtones, and many Jewish intellectuals, condemned as Zionists or 'rootless cosmopolitans', disappeared in the arid cultural deserts of the *Zhdanovshchina*.

In a sense the intense philistinism, paranoia, and xenophobia of this post-war period of 'high Stalinism' was an internal reflection of the rapidly deteriorating relations between the Soviet Union and the west in the early years of the Cold War.

Cold War

Rivers of ink have flowed in an attempt to trace and analyse the origins of the Cold War, which has in many ways dominated the course of international relations throughout the world since 1945. Many regional conflicts in far-flung areas of the globe are impossible to understand except in the context of the political, ideological, and military confrontation between the Soviet Union and her allies on the one hand and the United States and the western powers on the other. How did the wartime allies become peacetime antagonists?

Many would trace the origins of the Cold War right back to the Bolshevik Revolution of 1917, which the capitalist countries regarded as a direct threat to their own political stability and economic security. (Hence Churchill's call to throttle the infant monster, mentioned earlier.) In this interpretation, the wartime alliance was a temporary aberration forced on the participating countries by the shared menace of German Nazism, and the post-war slide into non-belligerent hostility merely a resumption of 'normal' relations. While there is much force in this argument, one must also seek the more immediate causes of the mutual suspicion, mistrust, and animosity during the last few years of Stalin's life.

At the conferences of Teheran and Yalta, as already indicated, some kind of loose agreement was reached among the 'Big Three' on the settlement of post-war Europe. It was understood that the Soviet Union had a legitimate interest in ensuring that the countries along her western and south-western borders should not only come within the USSR's 'sphere of influence', but also be governed by regimes which would be politically at least well-disposed to their eastern neighbour. If it is true that Stalin overestimated the degree of latitude he had in interfering in the internal politics of the east-European states, it is equally true that the explicitly hostile declarations of some western politicians, as well as Russia's long experience of vulnerability to invasion from the west, made Stalin unwaveringly determined that the military security of the USSR should have absolute priority over the political independence of those countries, some of which had in any case recently fought alongside Hitler. In this way, starting with eastern Germany and Poland, Stalin gradually extended direct Soviet political control over most of central and eastern Europe, thereby creating a *cordon sanitaire* or protective barrier of buffer states between the Soviet Union and the west. This was the famous 'Iron Curtain' across Europe, stretching from the Baltic to the Black Sea, about which Winston Churchill thundered in his speech at Fulton, Missouri, in 1946, which has often been interpreted as the west's opening verbal salvo of the Cold War.

In fact there had been more than a whiff of grape-shot about soon after the Yalta conference during an open confrontation in Washington between the new American President, Harry Truman (Roosevelt died in April 1945), and the Soviet Foreign Minister, Stalin's old crony from the Tsaritsyn days, Vyacheslav Molotov. In what one commentator described as 'the language of a Missouri mule-driver', Truman publicly harangued his visiting Soviet ally over what he regarded as the unacceptable composition of the proposed government of Poland, on which a compromise agreement had already been reached at Yalta. There was a heated exchange, but Stalin immediately wrote to the President in remarkably restrained tones pointing out the Soviet Union's crucial interest in ensuring the existence of a friendly government in adjacent Poland, and reminding him, correctly, that the USSR had neither been consulted about, nor claimed the right to interfere in, the establishment of the governments of, for instance, Greece or Belgium in the western sphere. 'To put it plainly,' he wrote, 'you want me to renounce the interests of the security of the Soviet Union; but I cannot proceed against the interests of my own country.' Stalin's face-to-face meeting with Truman at the Potsdam conference in July–August 1945 did nothing to dispel the mounting antipathy between the two formally allied leaders; indeed it served only to confirm their suspicions about each other's hostile intentions and drive them into even more firmly entrenched positions. Well before Churchill's Iron Curtain speech, therefore, the tone of the Cold War had been established.

On 6 and 9 August 1945, the United States of America dropped atomic bombs on the Japanese cities of Hiroshima and Nagasaki. It is impossible here to explore the complex web of military, political, moral, and technological arguments surrounding Truman's personal decision to use these dreadful new weapons of war. There is, however, an abundance of evidence to suggest that the decision was motivated as much by political considerations in relation to the Soviet Union as by military objectives against Japan. Even before the bomb was successfully tested, Truman had remarked, with reference to the Russians, *not* the Japanese, 'If it explodes . . . I'll have a hammer on those boys!' The American Secretary of State, James Byrnes, was also quite explicit in his opinion that the United States' possession and demonstration of the bomb 'would make Russia more manageable in Europe'.

He was wrong. If anything, it made Stalin even more intransigent in his determination to strengthen his hold on eastern Europe. Between 1946 and 1949 communist-dominated puppet governments were systematically imposed on East Germany, Poland, Czechoslovakia, Hungary, Romania, and Bulgaria, as the western allies joined the United States in its vigorous campaign to 'contain' the spread of communism across Europe at almost any cost. In the case of Yugoslavia, Marshal Tito's ideological break with Stalin in 1948 suggested that disunity within the Soviet bloc was capable of being encouraged, extended, and exploited to Stalin's disadvantage. In this way the so-called 'Truman Doctrine' of 'containment' gradually gave way to the policy of 'roll-back' – that is, an attempt to undermine the Soviet Union's monopoly of power in her 'satellite' countries and overthrow their communist governments. Some western statesmen even privately advocated the use of nuclear weapons to bring this about – not so much a policy of 'roll-back' as of 'wipe-out'! Stalin's response was a series of purges, arrests, proscriptions, trials, and even executions of east-European politicians suspected of anti-Soviet leanings or 'Titoist' sympathies, and to impose his own brand of socialism through terror everywhere east of the River Elbe.

In 1949 two important events took place. The first was the formation of the North Atlantic Treat Organization (NATO), a formal military alliance of eleven west-European and North American powers directed specifically against the Soviet bloc; the second was the victory of the communist revolution in China and the establishment of the Chinese People's Republic. Although the Soviet Union had played no part in Mao Tse-tung's triumph, the fact that the territorially largest and the demographically most populous countries in the world were now both governed by communist dictatorships added to the alarm of the capitalist powers and their Third World colonial dependencies in Asia and elsewhere. The Cold War had now shifted from being a conflict over spheres of influence in Europe to a global confrontation between two military super-powers and their respective allies, both of them armed, from 1953 onwards, with the hydrogen bomb and both, therefore, with the potential power to plunge the entire planet into a nuclear holocaust.

Although both Stalin and Truman may have misinterpreted each other's military intentions and/or capabilities in the early stages of the Cold War, this is the awesome responsibility they left their political heirs to shoulder when they both, in their different ways, departed from the political scene in 1953.

Death

Stalin's seventieth birthday was celebrated in December 1949 amidst extravagant outpourings of official encomia, obsequious greetings, exhibitions, publications, poetry, and even prayers. Apart from the ritual references to the various manifestations of his superlative leadership and genius, the more effusive offerings contained intimations of immortality. But not even Stalin was able to organize that. His mental condition was deteriorating and the last years of his life were spent shuttling between his office in the Kremlin and his country house, or *dacha*, just outside Moscow, surrounded by the members of his Politburo and personal entourage. Stalin worked mainly at night and his subordinates were expected to follow suit. They were also compelled to participate in the regular parties and heavy drinking sessions to which he had become increasingly addicted and which often featured music, dancing, crude practical jokes, and drunken horseplay. The picture of Stalin at this time which emerges from Khrushchev's later memoirs is graphically described by their editor as

the degeneration of this Attila figure into a broken and paranoid old man, scheming to destroy his closest colleagues before they destroyed him, afraid of the food from his own kitchens, but still striking terror into the hearts of all around him.

The most prominent people around him, who were later to form the so-called 'collective leadership' after Stalin's death, were Malenkov, Molotov, Kaganovich, Beria, Khrushchev, Mikoyan, and Voroshi-

56

lov, all of them plotting and scheming in an atmosphere of fear and mutual suspicion. The most senior member of the Politburo after Stalin himself, Andrei Zhdanov, had died, probably of natural causes, in 1948. He was replaced as head of the Leningrad party organization by Giorgii Malenkov, who seemed to be being groomed for the leadership succession. However, his authority was offset to some extent by the recall of Khrushchev from the post-war re-collectivization drive in the Ukraine and his appointment as head of the Moscow party organization. Beria, too, had a potentially formidable power base in the NKVD, although the fate of his two predecessors at its head, Yagoda and Yezhov, did not suggest that the position was exactly free of risk. From his Leningrad base, and with Stalin's obvious approval, Malenkov inaugurated a purge of senior party officials and Zhdanov protégés in order to consolidate his own position. The 'Leningrad Affair', as it came to be known, in fact spread far beyond Leningrad and resulted in the dismissal, arrest, and execution of an unknown number of people in the party and government hierarchy.

Proximity to Stalin was no guarantee of political survival or personal safety and there is a fair amount of evidence to suggest that around 1952 Stalin was on the verge of another major shake-up of personnel. In October of that year the Communist Party held its 19th Congress, the first for thirteen years. Stalin used the opportunity not only to alter the party statutes but also to disband the tightly-knit Politburo and replace it with a much larger, more amorphous policy-making body renamed the Praesidium. This at any rate implied a dilution of the authority of the old Politburo members, which could hardly have increased their sense of well-being. Added to this, some members of Molotov's and Mikoyan's family had been arrested; Stalin's long-serving personal secretary, the shadowy Poskrebyshev, had been dismissed; and even the odious Beria was under something of a cloud as a result of his mishandling of the affairs of his, and Stalin's, native Georgia. In eastern Europe, the trials of leading Communist Party officials were going ahead. Then in January 1953 came news of the 'Doctors' Plot'. It was announced that nine Kremlin doctors, most of them Jewish, had been arrested and accused of deliberately bringing about the death of Zhdanov in 1948 and of conspiring to assassinate a number of senior military figures. They were further charged with maintaining links with overseas intelligence agencies and international Jewish organizations. The echoes of the purges of the 1930s were unmistakable.

It seemed that Stalin was about to launch another wave of terror. However, if such was indeed his intention, he was prevented from carrying it through by the timely intervention of a fatal brain haemorrhage on 2 March 1953. He died three days later and the official bulletin solemnly announced that 'The heart of the wise leader and teacher of the Communist Party and the Soviet people – Joseph Vissarionovich Stalin – has ceased to beat.'

In her memoirs, Stalin's daughter, Svetlana Alliluyeva, describes the deathbed scene. Senior party men had hastily gathered at the *dacha* along with family members and household servants. When the final moment came, many of them, she says, including Malenkov, Khrushchev, Kaganovich, and other leading acolytes of the Stalin cult, shed genuine tears. It is not facetious to suggest that these tears, while genuine enough, may have been the expression not so much of grief as of relief. Whatever their innermost personal feelings at their master's demise, however, they now jointly faced the formidable task, as his political trustees, of administering the ambiguous and imponderable legacy of Stalin and Stalinism.

7

The ambiguous legacy

Joseph Stalin was General Secretary of the Soviet Communist Party for thirty-one years (1922–53). Over a similar period of time since his death there have been six others (Malenkov, Khrushchev, Brezhnev, Andropov, Chernenko and Gorbachev). During those years an enormous number of changes – economic, social, administrative, technological, cultural, and military – have taken place. The sum total of these changes is often described as a process of *de-Stalinization*; in other words an undoing, a dismantling or restructuring of the system and the machinery for running it which Stalin created. Before discussing to what extent the term is accurate or even appropriate, it is first necessary to decide what is meant by Stalin*ism*.

Stalinism

In his superb analysis of the origins and consequences of Stalinism, the Soviet historian Roy Medvedev tells us that he chose the title of his book, *Let History Judge*, as an indication of the inchoate nature of the proper, academic investigation of the Stalin cult, particularly in the Soviet Union where it took place. That was over twenty years ago, in 1968. Despite mountains of affidavits, accusations, eyewitness accounts, and material exhibits, history has not yet pronounced its final verdict, although more and more evidence is coming to light on which a better-informed, objective, and ideologically untrammelled judgement may one day be passed. It is, however, possible to identify a number of the specific features of Stalinism, which, when fitted together, produce a kind of imperfect, Identikit picture of a unique phenomenon.

First and foremost, there is the 'command economy' and the emphasis on heavy industry. From the inauguration of the first five-year plan and the collectivization of agriculture, every single aspect of economic life and financial activity in the Soviet Union is controlled, or at any rate is *supposed* to be controlled, by the state. This is not just a matter of setting production targets or working out an annual budget. Even in free-enterprise economies, it is ultimately the government which decides fiscal policies and also decides on such things as whether industries and public services should be nationally or privately owned, whether students should receive grants or loans and patients pay for medical treatment. To that extent, central direction of economic priorities is also a feature of capitalist economies. Under the Stalinist-type command economy, however, the state planning authorities and the various centralized ministries are theoretically in charge of the *entire* economic system, from deciding the size of the national defence budget and industrial investment priorities to establishing wage levels, prices, rents, bus fares, food subsidies, pensions, kindergarten fees, and funeral expenses. There are no such things as private banks, commercial advertising, stocks and shares, insurance firms, or limited companies. A small amount of private trade is legally tolerated – for instance, collective farmers can sell the produce grown on their personal allotments at the local market – but even this facility is at the discretion of the state and can therefore be curtailed, extended, or withdrawn by the government authorities. Thus, although the *kolkhozniki* are not technically state employees, they are nevertheless subject to central direction and state control. There is, of course, a huge black market, without which, it has been suggested, the command economy simply would not work; indeed, to some extent it even relies on its illegal operation, in the same way that parasites are often essential to the health of the body that hosts them. Otherwise, everyone, from Communist Party official to circus clown, is an employee of the state.

The second, and in a sense perhaps most glaringly obvious, feature of the system is what Khrushchev described as the 'cult of personality'; that is,

the elevation of one person, his transformation into a superman possessing supernatural characteristics, akin to those of a god.

Such a man supposedly knows everything, sees everything, thinks for everyone, can do anything, is infallible in his behaviour.

'Such a belief about Stalin', continues Khrushchev, 'was cultivated among us for many years.' Enough has already been said in the preceding pages to give an idea of the extraordinary, unprecedented proportions of the Stalin cult during his own lifetime. Two quotations will suffice here to illustrate the absurd nature of the adulation heaped upon him. The first is from Alexander Solzhenitsyn's novel *The First Circle*:

His image, more than any other human likeness in history, had been graven in stone, painted in oils, in water colour, in gouache and in sepia, drawn in charcoal, chalk and brickdust, patterned in gravel, seashells, glazed tiles, grains of wheat and soya beans, carved in ivory, grown in grass, woven in carpets, registered on celluloid and outlined in the sky by planes.

The second is a poem, or hymn, published in *Pravda* in 1936:

O great Stalin, O leader of the peoples,
Thou who broughtest man to birth,
Thou who fructifiest the earth,
Thou who restorest the centuries,
Thou who makest bloom the spring,
Thou who makest vibrate the chords of music . . .
Thou, splendour of my spring, O Thou,
Sun reflected by millions of hearts . . .

The third, and more sinister, feature is the operation of the police state and the implementation of rule through terror. Again, earlier chapters have referred to the various manifestations of NKVD activity with which Stalin maintained his tyrannical rule. The whole ghastly business of denunciation, arrest, interrogation, torture, imprisonment, exile, concentration camps, and executions to which many millions of people fell victim under Stalin was an essential and indispensable element of his system of political coercion and social control.

Fourth, there is what might be called the 'mobilized society'. This is something we are familiar with in times of total war, when not only the armed forces but every section of society is geared in some way towards the achievement of the national goal – in this case the defeat of the enemy. Under Stalinism, in peacetime as in war, each individual citizen of the Soviet Union was recruited, educated, trained, exhorted, regimented, and ultimately coerced into fulfilling his or her patriotic/political duty in the great historical task of building socialism and marching under Stalin's banner towards the ultimate victory of communism. Even schoolchildren were encouraged to report to the authorities members of their family, their own parents, if they overheard disloyal or critical opinions voiced in the dubious privacy of the home.

Fifth, Stalinism sought to regiment not just the bodies but also the minds of the population. This was not just a case of toeing the party political line on ideological issues. It involved the whole apparatus of literary censorship, political control of education and scholarship, conformity to centrally imposed artistic norms, and a total ban on all manifestations of intellectual individualism, unorthodoxy, or dissent. Cultural standardization and uniformity manifested itself not only in creative literature, but also in painting, music, theatre, ballet, and even architecture – the great leader favouring the gigantic monstrosities built in the 'Stalin baroque' style of which the central building of Moscow State University is a prime example.

Finally, although the list is not of course exhaustive, a characteristic feature of Stalinism, which is shared with other examples of totalitarianism, is its rampant nationalism. The emphasis on Soviet patriotism, which was barely distinguishable from *Great Russian* nationalism, went far beyond the simple love of country, and in gross distortion of the internationalist principles of original Marxism and Leninism took on the most unsavoury and obnoxious features of chauvinism, racial discrimination, anti-Semitism, a crude contempt for other cultural values, and a dangerous xenophobia which made even talking to foreigners a criminal offence.

Some or all of these features of Stalinism (and, to repeat, they do not form an exhaustive list) can be found to a greater or lesser extent in other examples of totalitarian regimes – Hitler's Germany, Mussolini's Italy, Pinochet's Chile, Mao's China, and Pol Pot's Kampuchea, for instance – but the peculiar blend in which they were to be found in Stalin's USSR makes his a distressingly unique and, one hopes, unrepeatable model.

De-Stalinization

Very soon after the dictator's death, various component parts of his system were subjected to a number of uncoordinated modifications and reforms which attenuated some of its harsher aspects. The universally detested Beria was arrested and shot, and the recently renamed KGB (Committee for State Security) placed firmly under party control. So far as we know, Beria's was the last political execution to have taken place in the Soviet Union. (So determined was the new leadership to have him 'unpersoned' that even overseas subscribers to the *Great Soviet Encyclopaedia* were sent instructions to cut out his biographical entry in volume 5, and replace it with a new set of pages containing an extended article on the Bering Strait!) In domestic policies a greater emphasis was given to the manufacture of consumer goods, an extensive housing programme was launched, collective farmers were granted more concessions and incentives, and the first, faint stirrings of a cultural 'thaw' began to be felt. Many of the purge victims who had managed to stay alive were released from the camps and began to pick up the pieces of their shattered lives.

In the realm of foreign policy there was a shift away from an insistence on the inevitability of military confrontation between capitalism and socialism and a revival of the old Leninist principle of 'peaceful coexistence'. Comradely overtures were made to Tito's Yugoslavia, and the Soviet government and party leaders Bulganin and Khrushchev (known to the west as 'B & K') embarked on a series of visits to capitalist countries (including Britain), something that Stalin had never done.

There was still no actual official policy that was called 'de-Stalinization' and no public acknowledgement that there was to be any radical departure from established procedures and attitudes. But then, in 1956, Nikita Khrushchev dropped a bombshell among the ranks of the party faithful. At the 20th Party Congress he delivered his famous 'secret speech' in which he attacked the 'cult of personality' and informed his dumbstruck audience that, far from being the wise and beneficent object of their earlier adulation, Stalin was in fact a bloodthirsty, criminal tyrant who had trampled on Leninist principles, overthrown standards of socialist legality, and sent thousands of innocent party comrades to their doom. It is difficult to convey the full impact of Khrushchev's dramatic revelations, but the shock-waves reverberated throughout the party, the country, the Eastern bloc, and the world communist movement. It was rather as if a Pope had denied the Virgin Birth and Resurrection, and officially declared to a Vatican Council that Jesus Christ was not the Son of God but a murderer, a charlatan, and a crook.

At any rate the 'secret speech' was a major turning-point in the history of the Soviet Union and led to a spate of liberalizing policies and intensified reforms. Stalin himself was now subjected to the same process of 'depersonification' as his previous victims and his name all but eradicated from the textbooks. Stalingrad was renamed Volgograd, and in 1961 his body was unceremoniously removed from Lenin's side in the mausoleum and buried beneath the Kremlin wall. Khrushchev even suggested that there should be a commission of inquiry into Stalin's crimes and a public monument to his victims.

De-Stalinization was, however, an ambiguous process. It was being implemented, after all, by men who had made their political careers out of blindly obeying his will. Stalinists were attempting to dismantle Stalinism, and there were in any case many still around in influential positions who thought things had gone far enough in the direction of liberalization and reform. In 1964 Khrushchev was himself ousted from office and succeeded by a team of bureaucrats headed by Leonid Brezhnev (1906–82), who presided over almost two more decades of economic and cultural immobility which are now officially condemned as the 'era of stagnation'. Stalin was not rehabilitated, but his heinous crimes against humanity were conveniently dismissed as 'errors', 'deviations from Leninist norms', 'mistakes', and 'consequences of the personality cult'. Dissident intellectuals and critics, writers who circulated uncensored literature or published it abroad, 'anti-Soviet agitators', religious activists, and would-be emigrant Jews were subjected to a sustained campaign of official harassment and police persecution which resulted in the trial, imprisonment, confinement in psychiatric units, exile, or banishment of many whose only crime was to call attention to what they saw as the possibility of a return to the standards and practices of the Stalin period.

To some extent they had good reason to be alarmed. In terms of the various ingredients of Stalinism discussed above, apart from the cult of personality itself, there was still plenty of evidence of the command economy, the powers of the KGB, the mobilization of human resources in the interests of the state, cultural sterility, and intense national chauvinism. The blood-letting of the Great Terror was absent, but a powerful residue still remained of die-hard attitudes and institutions, behavioural patterns, economic and military priorities, and knee-jerk responses to external stimuli which were all part of the mindless, conditioned-reflex system of 'classical' Stalinism.

Glasnost

At the time of writing (1989) it is less than half a decade since Mikhail Gorbachev took over the post of party General Secretary which Stalin made so powerful. In those few years a tremendous sea-change has come about in the Soviet Union on which it is much too soon for a historian to pass judgement. However, the ripples set in motion by Khrushchev's attack on the cult of personality which then disappeared during the years of Brezhnevite stagnation have now grown into waves which are billowing and surging with as yet untold consequences. Ancient taboos are being broken, old outcasts are being rehabilitated, and hidden skeletons in the gloomy cupboard of Soviet history are being brought into the light of public and academic scrutiny.

More tragically and dramatically, real skeletons of thousands of Stalin's victims have recently been unearthed from mass graves in Byelorussia and the Ukraine. Surviving eyewitnesses have revealed to the press their memories of the long nights of terror as the forests reverberated with the continuous sound of NKVD gunfire, and there have been public calls for the perpetrators of those horrors who are still alive to be hunted down and tried in the same way as Nazi war criminals. In Moscow an officially approved organization called Memorial, funded by public donation and bequest, has been established to investigate the crimes of Stalin and to raise a monument to the memory of his victims. Those who would not, could not, or dared not speak out in the past are now enjoying the opportunities of *glasnost* to pursue their investigations in the full glare of publicity. The works of foreign scholars who have written of the Stalinist past are now openly published and their authors fêted in newspaper columns and the lecture theatres of Soviet universities. In 1988 Nikolai Bukharin was officially rehabilitated by a judicial inquiry and posthumously restored to party membership, a great source of comfort to his surviving widow. The economic treatises of this major champion of NEP are now on public sale and it is now even possible to read dispassionate articles discussing the historical role of Trotsky in terms that would have been until recently unthinkable.

At a meeting of the party Central Committee in 1989, Gorbachev himself roundly condemned the atrocities committed in the drive to collectivize the peasantry during the 1930s and he has also used his authority to call on writers and historians to fill in the blank pages in

Russia's recent past – pages on which their predecessors were too craven, ignorant, or obsequious to write.

In short, it seems that the malign spirit of Joseph Vissarionovich Stalin, which has haunted the Soviet Union since his death, is about to be cast out. It remains to be seen whether Mikhail Gorbachev will have proved to be an effective and successful exorcist, or whether the ghost will return.

Suggestions for further reading

The literature on Stalin is enormous in quantity and varied in quality. The following is a highly selective list (in alphabetical order of author's name) of some of the more interesting, useful, and respectable works on Stalin, Stalinism, and the Stalinist period of Soviet history. Reference to further material is contained in the notes and bibliographies to most of these volumes.

S. Alliluyeva, *Twenty Letters to a Friend* (London, 1967).
H. Carrère d'Encausse, *Lenin: Revolution and Power* (London, 1982).
—*Stalin: Order through Terror* (London, 1981).
S. F. Cohen, *Bukharin and the Russian Revolution: A Political Biography* (Oxford, 1980).
R. Conquest, *The Great Terror* (London, 1968).
R. V. Daniels (ed.), *The Stalin Revolution: Foundations of Soviet Totalitarianism* (Lexington and Toronto, 1972).
I. Deutscher, *Stalin: A Political Biography* (London, 1966).
—*The Prophet Unarmed: Trotsky, 1921–1929* (Oxford, 1970).
M. Djilas, *Conversations with Stalin* (London, 1962).
J. Erickson, *The Road to Stalingrad* (London, 1975).
S. Fitzpatrick, *The Russian Revolution, 1917–1932* (Oxford, 1982).
E. Ginzburg, *Into the Whirlwind* (London, 1968).
G. Hosking, *A History of the Soviet Union* (London, 1985).
N. S. Khrushchev, *Khrushchev Remembers* (London, 1971) – contains text of Khrushchev's 'secret speech'.

M. McCauley, *Stalin and Stalinism* (London, 1983).

R. H. McNeal, *Stalin: Man and Ruler* (London, 1988).

R. A. Medvedev, *Let History Judge: The Origins and Consequences of Stalinism* (Oxford, 1989).

—*On Stalin and Stalinism* (Oxford, 1979).

A. Nove, *An Economic History of the USSR* (London, 1969).

—*Stalinism and After* (London, 1975).

R. Pethybridge, *The Social Prelude to Stalinism* (London, 1975).

A. Solzhenitsyn, *The Gulag Archipelago*, 3 vols (London, 1974, 1975, and 1978).

J. V. Stalin, *Leninism* (London, 1940).

L. Trotsky, *The Revolution Betrayed* (London, 1967).

—*The Stalin School of Falsification* (New York, 1962).

R. C. Tucker, *Stalin as Revolutionary, 1879–1929* (London, 1974).

—(ed.), *Stalinism: Essays in Historical Perspective* (New York, 1977).

One may also read with profit Arthur Koestler's brilliant novel *Darkness at Noon* (London, 1940).